BARGAINING GAMES

ALSO BY J. KEITH MURNIGHAN

The Dynamics of Bargaining Games

BARGAINING
GAMES

A NEW
APPROACH
TO STRATEGIC
THINKING IN
NEGOTIATIONS

J. KEITH MURNIGHAN

William Morrow and Company, Inc.
New York

It is the policy of William Morrow and Company, Inc., and its imprints and affiliates, recognizing the importance of preserving what has been written, to print the books we publish on acid-free paper, and we exert our best efforts to that end.

Library of Congress Cataloging-in-Publication Data

Murnighan, John Keith.
    Bargaining games: a new approach to strategic thinking in
negotiations / by J. Keith Murnighan.
        p.   cm.
    ISBN 0-688-10905-5
    1. Negotiation. 2. Negotiation in business. I. Title.
    BF637.N4M8   1992
    302.3—dc20   91-48048
                                                                                CIP

Printed in the United States of America

First Edition

1 2 3 4 5 6 7 8 9 10

BOOK DESIGN BY PATRICE FODERO

For Mom and Dad
and Jack and Erik

CONTENTS

BARGAINING GAMES

CHAPTER 1

FIRST THINGS FIRST

You have decided that it's time to buy a new car. You've kept your eyes open lately and think you know what you want. In fact, there's one model that has really caught your eye. You can't help being excited about the possibility of actually owning and driving this car.

You decide to check it out with a dealer. The test drive is just fine—it really feels good. As you expected, however, the price is not as low as you would like it to be. After some haggling (and possibly checking out a few other cars), you make the deal and buy the car. You feel a great rush—what a car!

The big question is whether you got a good deal. I have never met anyone who has just bought a car who believes he made a bad deal. *Everyone* thinks he got a bargain. If something goes wrong with the car soon afterward, he may change his mind. But *immediately* after the purchase, everyone feels that he got a good deal.

Most people think this way, and think that they are good bargainers. They also believe that they are more honest and more ethical than most people. Not only that, people typically think that they are better drivers than other people and that their chances of contracting cancer or being hit by a car are less than most other people's. All this reflects the simple fact that

11

most of us suffer from illusions of control. We think that we control our lives more than we actually do. (In fact, this feeling of being in control helps keep us mentally healthy.)

If we return to the fact that we all believe we get a good deal when we buy a car, we clearly have a problem. How can all of us get a good deal when we buy a car? How would so many car dealers ever stay in business? The unhappy fact is that we don't always come away with a bargain. Indeed, we rarely find out whether we have made a good deal or a bad one. Ironically, this lack of knowledge allows us to tell ourselves that we made a wise purchase. If we really knew how everything was going to turn out, we might not be so happy. The main point here is that there is a lot of room for people to improve their bargaining skills.

Bargaining Games is obviously about bargaining. At the same time, it is about life. Bargain well and your life will be better—and much of the time other people's lives will also improve. Since everyone bargains all the time, all of us can gain by being better bargainers.

This book is about cooperation and competition and everything in between. I once heard a story about Chinese heaven and Chinese hell that illustrates the difference quite simply. If you should wind up in Chinese hell, you will find that everyone has chopsticks that are thirty feet long and no one can feed himself. If, on the other hand, you are fortunate enough to wind up in Chinese heaven, you will also find that everyone has thirty-foot chopsticks. But, in Chinese heaven, everyone feeds each other.

Part of the value of this story comes from the realization that it takes work to get cooperation going and more work to keep it going. Competition, on the other hand, is what people naturally slide into. It can be and often is almost a natural reaction to conflict or negotiations. Most interactions include the possibility for both competition and cooperation. They are what we call *bargaining games:* interactions where each party can be strategically cooperative or competitive, or both.

The stories I will tell about these games should help prepare you for many different negotiations. The vicarious experiences they provide and your own thoughtful analysis of the games should help improve your bargaining strategies and your bargaining intuitions. After reading *Bargaining Games,* you should know more about how to approach a negotiation; you should be less troubled by the fear and anxiety many people experience when they are forced to negotiate.

Each chapter will give you a new outlook on how to bargain for a car (our basic example) or on how to negotiate in general. The subtleties of different situations are critical, but there are many clear lessons to be learned from different bargaining games. They include:

How the starting price can affect the final outcome

How your emotions and your opponent's contribute to the process

How verbal and nonverbal messages indicate interest or reveal that someone is lying

How information is critical before and during negotiations

When threats and ultimatums are effective—or when they're disastrous

When a third person can help others reach a deal that is better than what they could get without intervention

When and why things sometimes get out of control

Whether, when, and why it sometimes pays to volunteer

How easy it is to get involved in a costly bidding war

How you and an opponent can get as much from a deal as possible

How your negotiation might affect people not directly involved

Whether you can trust an adversary enough to reveal what you would really want from a deal

How fair and ethical you and others might be as you bargain

Bargaining Games will help you know yourself better as a bargainer. You will be able to use that self-knowledge automatically. You'll be in a much better position to negotiate—almost anything, almost anytime.

A TRUE CAR STORY

My ex-wife's uncle once came home and announced that he had gotten a great deal on the new car he had just bought. For a long time he and his wife had not owned a car. They lived in the city and used public transportation. But their circumstances changed and it became clear that they needed a car. So he went to a dealer and, that very first day, he bought a new car! He didn't go to see any other dealers. He didn't consider other models. He didn't check out the used car market. He didn't read any consumer magazines. But he arrived home with his new set of wheels and triumphantly announced that he had gotten a great deal.

I was quietly skeptical at the time. I knew little about bargaining then, and less about cars, but I couldn't imagine that he had just walked into the wonderful bargain he was claiming. He just couldn't have prepared enough; there was no way that he had gathered enough information to bargain well. Instead of finding such a good deal, I couldn't help thinking, he probably had made one car dealer very happy that day.

Bargaining games, simply defined, are strategic interactions. They can be playful (for example, card and board games) or serious (military leaders playing games of war). Bargaining games are employed in strategic situations where bargaining is expected, where the people involved must act strategically, where competition and/or cooperation can reign. One of the most basic of bargaining games, as you have probably guessed, is the game of buying a car. I'll use it as an example throughout the book.

Effective bargaining serves everyone well. Consider collective bargaining, the labor-management ritual that many people think of as being very antagonistic. Collective bargaining does include competition, but it also has many cooperative elements. The chief negotiators, for instance, must make sure that they can sell whatever agreement they reach to their constituents. If the agreement is lopsided and favors one side or the other too much, it won't be approved and the negotiators will have to go back and begin again. In addition, both sides must live with each other on a daily basis after they have agreed on a contract, so they both must be reasonably satisfied with it. Neither side wants the other to be so unhappy that they need to take out their disgruntlements day after day. Contracts run for a long time; when they are based on mutual respect and cooperation, they make smooth internal functioning and superior performance possible. And, finally, getting down to the bottom line, if the union does too well in a negotiation, the company may go broke; if management does too well, the best workers may find better-paying jobs elsewhere. Even in the most competitive atmosphere, cooperation can provide many mutual benefits. Bargaining well, then, means that you must not only consider the desired outcome for your own side; you must also consider the outcome desired by others.

Effective bargaining takes practice. I've never met a born negotiator. Children are the exception to this statement: Parents know how well they negotiate. It's because they are so persistent. By the time they go through adolescence, though, they typically lose their ability to bargain, probably because they have learned to fear embarrassment. Thus, as adults, we need to learn how to bargain all over again. We do have the advantage, though, of being able to learn additional, more complex strategies.

Bargaining Games will make you a better bargainer by presenting you with a variety of games. As I discuss the story surrounding each game, you should visualize what you would do if you were about to play that game. As each story unfolds, you will see what other people actually did. Sometimes you will analyze the game well and predict how things turned out. Even better will be the times when you discover the optimal bargaining strategy. But those times may be relatively rare. My guess is that, for many of the games, you will be surprised either by what happened or what should have happened.

Strategic thinking is one of the keys to good negotiation. Implementation is the other. Both are essential for a successful negotiation—unless you are very lucky. If you formulate good strategies and implement them well, you will be very successful, almost by definition. The problem is determining what strategies are best and how to implement them before you begin bargaining. After a negotiation, analyzing what happened is very important—but it's much better to be poised and ready before you begin. That's where intuition comes in, and that's where I hope this book will have a big impact. Practice, experience, and thinking can inform your intuitions so that you can react quickly and effectively when bargaining games present themselves. This sounds simple enough. As you will see, however, a multitude of strategies is possible in any negotiation; their effectiveness may turn on split-second timing or a subtle phrase or gesture. Bargaining can be very easy—especially when you do it badly! Effective bargaining requires serious thought, careful analysis, and lots of practice. But as you will see, it can also be challenging and enjoyable.

People who are actively involved in research on negotiations (like me) see bargaining everywhere. Many examples are obvious: interviewing for a job, buying something at an antique show, searching out the best price for a diamond ring, the give-and-take of international diplomacy, a teenager wanting to use the family car on Saturday night, and labor-management relations. Many other interactions can benefit from a bargaining perspective; two people meeting for the first time and, during their conversation, subtly negotiating whether their future interactions will be romantic, businesslike, or nonexistent; the runners in a 1,500-meter race negotiating lanes and surges with their elbows or their feet, trying to be in the best position at the finish; executives who need a gargantuan task completed immediately, but who present it to their secretaries with a smile, saying, "Could you possibly handle this?" Numerous transactions between wives and husbands, parents and children, employers and employees, and sets of acquaintances and friends are similarly negotiated. Although all of these people may not be bargaining explicitly, we can learn quite a lot about their interactions by thinking of them as bargaining.

Before I go further in introducing this book, I'd like to tell a story about an unusual bargaining interaction. It's one with a surprise solution. At the same time, it exemplifies the interpersonal analysis that's so important in bargaining games.

AN UPSIDE-DOWN EXAMPLE

Recently I was teaching my MBA course on bargaining. The course was horrendously overenrolled—there were over eighty people in the class. As a result, no one had a chance to ask questions about their everyday bargaining problems. To alleviate this situation, I instituted "Almost Free Negotiation Consulting." Each Monday afternoon at five o'clock I would go to a prearranged local bar and buy myself a beer. If students wanted to raise questions about bargaining, they had to make sure that I didn't run out of beer—that's why the consulting was "almost" free.

One afternoon one of my best students, let's call him Rick, was among the group. After telling us how he had negotiated badly and probably paid too much for a beat-up old convertible that he truly loved, he raised an intriguing question. Rick was graduating soon and had just finished a round of final interviews with several companies. He was very pleased because the company he wanted to work for had made him an offer; he was going to take it. The salary they offered was good, but he had a nagging feeling that it could be better. He wanted to ask them for more money before he accepted the job, but he didn't want to alienate them in any way because he fully intended to accept the job, even if they couldn't or didn't offer him any additional money.

Rick's immediate priority was to be accepted by the people in the firm. The starting salary was secondary: He wanted to deal with it if he could, but he wanted to be very careful. He didn't want the salary issue to interfere with a smooth transition into the job. How could he increase his chances for a better salary without turning off anyone at the company?

Normally, salary negotiations are strictly distributive: The company either keeps a little more of its money or it *distributes* some of it to you. Distributive bargaining is often very competitive. When labor and management bargain over wages, for instance, it's usually tooth and nail, nose to nose.

But Rick's circumstances were different—salary wasn't the most important issue. As a result, the strategy we discussed and that was finally recommended was exactly the opposite of the obvious one. Rather than asking for more money before he accepted the job—with the expectation that he would then get involved in potentially difficult negotiations—he simply accepted the job and said how happy he was to be coming to the firm. (That was completely true.) Then he said that there was one thing troubling him—the starting salary. He couldn't help feeling that it was a little low. (That was also true.) Could they do something about it?

This strategy restructured the entire interaction. Rather than taking an aggressive, distributive bargaining stand, as many people think they must in salary negotiations, Rick shook hands first, accepted the job, and then asked the firm, as a matter of good faith, to help on the salary issue. He didn't beg or plead or bargain hard—just the reverse. He agreed with them on the big issue and left his final salary—the issue that he had defined as secondary—up to them. He was already part of the team; it was now their turn. Rick's strategy opened the door for the company to reciprocate. He hoped that they would say to themselves, "Rick accepted, now it's our turn to do something." Rick's strategy also took the burden off his own shoulders and placed it squarely on the firm's: If they didn't come through, they would be the ones who looked bad.

Early the next day Rick proceeded just as planned. Someone from the company called him back a few hours later and said that they could increase his salary by $5,000. Needless to say,

Rick was very pleased. He even acknowledged that the beer he had bought me the night before was the best investment he had ever made.

This story is not unique. *Bargaining Games* assumes that different situations require different bargaining strategies. You would be bargaining poorly if you used the same negotiation techniques with your boss, your spouse, a merchant who sold you a faulty television set, the other four members of a pickup basketball team, or a police officer who pulled you over for rolling through a stop sign. Not only are different strokes needed for different folks, but different situations require different strategies, appropriately implemented.

THE OLD CITY

One day several years ago I was fortunate enough to be visiting the Old City in Jerusalem. It was packed with shops selling all sorts of wonderful and not so wonderful things. Negotiating was obviously the norm, the shopkeepers all spoke English, and the prices were stated in dollars. This was great! Exotic things to bargain for in a language and a currency I could understand. I felt like a sinner in heaven.

My first purchase was a funky wool bag, with colorful tassels and a shoulder strap. I honestly don't know why I bought it. It was one of those purposeless but intriguing purchases that travelers often buy while on vacation.

Afterward, when I was replaying the negotiation in my mind, I realized that I had paid too much. The bag wasn't expensive, but I did pay too much for it; I had bargained badly.

Here is what happened: During our haggling the seller made a bad mistake, but I was too busy thinking about how much I liked the bag and how much I would be willing to pay for it to notice. It only hit me afterward that he had said, "It's really old." There was *no possible way* that this bag was old: It was obviously a new product; it even smelled new.

I should have stopped the discussion, pointed out that the

bag was obviously new, and acted like I was offended (which is how I would have felt). He might have given up on the negotiation, knowing that he wasn't going to do very well anymore. If he did, I would have had to buy a similar bag elsewhere—armed with the knowledge I had gained from this first negotiation. If he still wanted to continue negotiating, I would have been in a very strong, unassailable position. If fact, by buying this bag, I made the same mistake my ex-wife's uncle made when he bought their first car—I didn't collect enough information before I finalized the deal. Instead, I purchased the first bag that I saw. Clearly, I didn't spend as much as Uncle Bill did on his car. Nevertheless, I had had plenty of time, and similar bags were probably available. It would have been better to do a little haggling and walk away. That works very well if you know you can buy the object later, especially from someone else. The only costs you incur with this strategy are time and effort and possibly alienating the seller. If it's a one-of-a-kind object or opportunity, though, leaving and coming back tells the seller that you're *very* interested.

I did learn an important lesson from this interaction. I would have to be very careful in the Old City: The sellers were not above what we think of in America as unethical tactics. Luckily this was a lesson that didn't cost much.

I wandered around all day, buying various gifts for relatives and friends or treats for myself. At one of the shops, I saw a fairly crude but colorful rug. The salesman there used the same line that so many of the shopkeepers were using at the time: "It doesn't cost anything to look." I asked him how much the rug would cost. His excellent strategic response was "How much do you want to pay?" I told him that I didn't want to pay anything; I really wasn't interested in the rug; I was just curious about its price. (That was true—I really didn't want the rug at all.)

After some discussion, he finally told me that the rug's price was $35. He also convinced me that I should reciprocate and tell him how much I would be willing to pay for it. I consciously chose a very low price, one that might actually tempt me to buy it. I told him $10. He responded by dragging me into the shop and showing me other rugs of lesser quality with lower prices, "since you can't afford to pay thirty-five dollars." I could afford the $35; I just wasn't that interested. I knew $35 was an inflated price designed for tourists like me. I did like the colorful rug, but I was only willing to pay $10 for it. In fact, I didn't really know I would actually pay $10 until somewhat later.

I told him what I was thinking. I had nothing to hide. He relented and said I could have it for $30. I continued to say I didn't really want it. He kept trying to show me less expensive rugs. We went back and forth. I was really having a good time; I still had no intention of buying the rug. I stayed at $10; his price kept dropping and dropping, but only slowly. I started to leave; he came down some more. Finally I said, "Okay. Thank you for your time—I've really enjoyed talking with you. But I'm going to leave now. I will go up to twelve dollars, but that's all." I was smiling and still enjoying myself a lot. He rubbed his chin, still tried to get me to pay more, but finally he surprised me and agreed. He tied up the rug, I walked off, and immediately I wondered not only what I was going to do with it, but also, how was I going to fit it in my suitcase?

A few minutes later I was walking by some other rug sellers. One saw my rug and said that I should *not* have bought a colorful rug. He said that the colors would run if it got wet and proceeded to demonstrate with one of his own colored rugs! He asked me how much I had paid for my rug. I said $10. (We will discuss the ethics of that statement later in the book.) He didn't believe me and asked again, "How much did you pay?" Again I said I paid $10. He continued to express disbelief and wouldn't accept the fact that I was happy with my rug and didn't want to trade it for one of his. Finally as I pried myself from his shop and started walking away, he called to me and said, "I'll sell you a rug for five dollars!" I just turned and waved and laughed at him. As I kept walking, a nearby shopkeeper touched my arm and said, "You should buy his rug. He's *never* sold a rug for five dollars before."

The negotiating techniques described in *Bargaining Games* are embedded in the folklore of stories like these. I would love to take a group of people to an actual market in the Middle East to test our techniques and see how well we could bargain.

Since that's not practical, I will tell you a bunch of stories about a variety of bargaining games. The games are simple and, as a result, their lessons apply to many different negotiations. In particular, they are designed to address the essentials of intuitive bargaining strategies, as well as the nuts and bolts of negotiations.

Be forewarned, however: Different bargaining situations may have very different sets of informal rules and constraints. Thus, blindly following my strategies from the Old City could lead to deep trouble in other negotiations. In the same way, Rick might have been badly hurt if he had followed the normal pattern of salary negotiations. If you think a lot about these games, your bargaining intuitions should improve to the point where you move automatically to the right kinds of strategies.

Throughout the book, I will touch on a variety of topics, including friendship, norms, reputations, and information. Each has a direct impact on the process and outcomes of bargaining. First and foremost, it's essential to pay attention to the three basic rules of bargaining. They are:

Know yourself.

Know the other person.

Know the situation.

Whenever you're bargaining you should try to determine what you really want to achieve. You should also think about how you want to feel when the negotiation is finished. To do this well, it's essential to know yourself. That is the sine qua non of successful negotiators. As Yogi Berra once said, "If you don't know what you want, you might not get it."

THE URGE TO COMPETE

A few rules of thumb will help you when you bargain. First, it's important to determine what you really want and how you can best obtain it. That sounds selfish but it doesn't have to be.

When you are trying to do as well as you can for yourself, part of what you might want can include what happens to everyone else. Thus, I am *not* advocating that you should always be competitive. On the contrary, you should *not* try to beat anyone else. Trying to beat the other person is usually very destructive—for you and everyone else. Let them get whatever they can. If you are negotiating and, at the same time, you're thinking about whether you will do better or worse than the other person, you will be putting the cart before the horse and you won't do as well. Knowing yourself helps you know what you want and can provide clues as to how to get it.

Competing (trying to beat the other person) is a disease that is very hard to eradicate. Over and over again, I've seen people miss a golden opportunity because they were afraid their opponent would do even better. This faulty thinking is pervasive in our competitive culture. It takes real effort to pause before enacting a competitive strategy to ask yourself whether you're choosing the *best* strategy or whether you're trying to beat the other bargainer. The desire to win is so deeply ingrained that many of us are unnecessarily competitive—and that can seriously hurt our ability to bargain well and to get the most, individually and/or jointly, out of an interaction.

In many negotiations, when you bargain well, you and everyone involved will obtain very good outcomes. But trying to beat someone else can be *mutually disastrous*—in so doing, you may hurt everyone, including yourself. Without going into great detail, we can easily imagine that wars often start because people or countries are overly competitive. Knowing the situation you are bargaining in is essential here. I will cover this in more depth throughout the book.

At different times in their lives, most people find themselves in a variety of different negotiations, sometimes favorable, sometimes not; at times cooperation is possible, at other times it is not. Knowing the situation and the other person can indicate how you stand before you begin so that you can *work within your own position*. When you find that you really need an agreement, for instance, and the other person doesn't, you may have to concede more to make sure that you do agree.

Thus, new-car dealers may offer a better buy on a car at the end of a month when they must meet a quota. Similarly, I probably had less interest in buying a rug in the Old City than either of the rug sellers had in selling one. Caring less usually gives one side an advantage. Other elements can also increase or decrease your power in a negotiation. Realizing when you are strong and when you are not is very important, and an issue we will be discussing later at greater length.

The people you bargain with will be trying to do as well as they can, too, from their own positions. Indeed, their situation may differ from yours; their resources may differ from yours; their information may differ from yours. In most negotiations, it's rare for you to ever find out how well the others did in your joint negotiations. Thus, it's important when you're negotiating to *make sure that you are happy* with your own outcome. My ex-wife's uncle was happy about the deal he got on his new car; because people think they get good deals when they buy a car, they feel happy when they end their negotiations. In some sense, that may be enough. As we've mentioned, it helps mental health.

But when we consider what might have happened with better bargaining, being happy is not enough. As outside observers, we can view this negotiation critically: We *know* that Uncle Bill could have done better. But just as in other fields, whether it is management or poker, art or athletics, the more you know, the more self-critical you can become. Thus, having more knowledge means that you may sacrifice some happiness. Once you get beyond ignorance, you may not always find bliss. On the other hand, being informed and knowledgeable means that you can improve your performance. Although it might take more to make you happy when you are well informed, your skills can help you get more out of a negotiation. Knowing more doesn't have to make you less happy if you use your knowledge to do better.

Most of the time we think of bargaining outcomes in terms of money. Not all bargaining games, however, can be so easily quantified. You wouldn't want to evaluate the outcomes for two people in a romantic interaction in terms of money. Money often does illustrate how different strategies work and what they can achieve. A word of caution, though: *Some negotiations should not be analyzed quantitatively.* Another story makes this point clearly.

BARGAINING IN REVERSE

My friend Lou and I were riding in his car one day, shortly after I had bought a house. I realized that there were lots of things that I needed now that I was a homeowner. One of those things, which I mentioned to Lou, was a vacuum cleaner. It so happened that he had just upgraded: His electric broom couldn't handle his new carpeting so he had recently purchased a fancy vacuum cleaner. He said, "Why don't I give you the electric broom?" I said, "No, I should buy it from you. I'll give you, oh, twenty-five dollars for it." He said, "No, give me ten." I said, "How about twenty?" He said, "Let's just settle on fifteen." That ended the negotiations. I bought his electric broom for $15.

On the face of it, this was a very strange negotiation. He was the seller and I was the buyer. Yet I continually offered *more* than he was asking and only dropped the price I offered as he raised the price he was willing to accept. Clearly, this was not the way that most sellers and buyers interact. We apparently got everything mixed up.

Underneath this negotiation of price, however, was an unspoken understanding that our friendship was much more important than the exchange of an electric broom. Lou no longer needed this electric broom; I could use it; he wanted me to have it. Our negotiation was a way for us to work out a scheme where I would be happy about his giving me something of obvious value as long as I gave him something, even if it was only a nominal amount. This bargain made us both laugh. But it was an efficient exchange of an electric broom and a little money. Most important, it reaffirmed our friendship. In this case the quantitative aspects of our bargaining were almost completely unimportant.

To improve your negotiation skills, you must occasionally step back from a negotiation and be sure you realize why you are bargaining and what the important issues are. Several of my friends have vacationed in Latin America. They are always intrigued by the local craftspeople who make all sorts of colorful pottery and paintings. They often come back with a story about having found a really lovely object priced at all of $2. In a gift shop or a gallery in the States, this prize would cost much, much more. Nevertheless, they learn that they are expected to haggle, so they automatically start bargaining, trying to drive the price all the way from $2.00 to $1.50 or even lower. Some of my friends have gotten the object home before they realized how ludicrous their bargaining was! Bargaining a little is important so that you don't come across as a stupid tourist; at the same time, however, paying somewhat more than the rock bottom minimum is usually not a problem. The extra 50 cents is almost meaningless to most of us; it may be very meaningful to the artist.

As in most negotiations like this, knowing yourself is critical: By realizing that the object and its purchase are more important to you than minuscule differences in price, you can make sure that you make the deal, that you get the object, and that you don't pay too little.

TWO MORE TIPS

1. Before you begin and whenever you are negotiating, try to stay calm and cool. Getting too emotionally involved, which is all too easy, will only blunt your ability to detect why other people are behaving the way they are and how they might be perceiving you. Getting too emotional blocks your ability to think clearly and creatively. Be calm, even though it can be very difficult.

There is at least one noteworthy exception to this rule, one time when you may not want to be calm, when it may be important to express anger. That is when the other party has violated your trust or has acted unethically, and you would prefer not dealing with them ever again. When you no longer care about the negotiation and you know you will never encounter the others again, you can vent your feelings with little cost and possibly some personal benefit. Indeed, they may even apologize and concede enough to resurrect your interaction. Chapter 3 discusses some of the other special cases where emotional outbursts are important. But those cases are rare. It's much better to stay cool, calm, and collected.

2. Do what you can to be perceived positively. Don't come across as someone whom people would just as soon not deal with. Even if you hold a powerful position, even if you will never see the other party again, you are best off (in most but not all situations) by not abusing your power. Realize that all bargains are exchanges and that it takes two to tango. At the very least, abusing power can damage your impression of yourself.

When I was working on my dissertation and applying for faculty positions around the country, I was contacted by the University of Illinois and asked to come for an interview. It was my first formal job interview. (As it turns out, it was also my last.) I was very nervous. This was a very good job at a very good school. I had secretly hoped that I could have interviewed at a smaller, less important school first, to get my professional feet wet. Instead, I spent a lot of time preparing for my interview. I worked and reworked my research presentation and read as much of the recent research of the Illinois faculty as I could find.

Before I left, one of my mentors gave me some terrific advice: He told me that the most important thing in an interview was to make sure they liked me. Certainly I needed to show that I knew what I was talking about. But the most important thing was personal—I should try to make sure that they liked me. I don't think he was saying that I should hide my true personality so that I could get this job—at least I hope not. Instead, he was telling me to be pleasant, outgoing, smile a little here and there—in general, to be someone that they would like to have as a colleague. The same advice applies in almost any bargaining situation: Being someone who's pleasant to bargain with will make your opponent happier, both during and after your negotiations, and paves the way for future interactions.

TEN BASIC RULES OF NEGOTIATING

Here are ten rules of thumb that should be applied in any negotiation.

1. Know yourself. Know what you are willing to do and what you are not willing to do when you bargain. Know how much value you place on the issues you will be negotiating. Are there principles involved that are tremendously important to you? How much do you really value the money that's involved? How do you feel about the other people in this interaction?

2. Do as well as you can for *you.* The other person will probably be doing the same, possibly more competitively. But if you both get what you want, you have probably done very well. You can hurt a potentially effective negotiation by not trying to do as well as you possibly can. If you know yourself, you should try to maximize what you want out of the negotiation.

3. Get as much information as you can before you begin. Buying a car is the easiest example where this rule of thumb applies.

4. Stay calm, cool, and collected. Act like a *professional* when you negotiate. Respect your own position, other people's positions, and the situation. Present yourself in a positive light. Expect and demand respect from the other parties.

5. Don't be competitive just for its own sake—you don't need to beat the other person to do well. Just satisfy yourself as much as you can. (This is essentially a rewarding of rule number 2.)

6. Differentiate among different bargaining games. Some call for competitive behavior; some work better if you're cooperative. Subtle changes in the situation can make a huge difference. Knowing when you can afford to pursue a cooperative strategy is tremendously important. (I will deal with this in subsequent chapters.)

7. Work within your own position. If you have little or no power, don't act as if you do. On the other hand, if you are blessed with power, you may not have to flaunt it to be effective.

8. The most important outcome of a negotiation may not be monetary. This reiterates rule 1, with a mix of rule 3. Realize what is important to you in the situation and do as much for yourself as you can.

9. Think strategically. What should you do next? What is the other person saying now and what do his or her words and actions suggest, indicate, or imply? Afterward, evaluate your performance. Were your strategies effective? How could you have done better? Analyzing your results and providing yourself with feedback can be very important in getting ready for future negotiations.

10. The tenth commandment: Once it's over, it's over. (This is a paraphrase of another Yogi Berra quote.) Don't worry about outcomes that you didn't achieve. It's enough to know that you were actively thinking while you negotiated and that you can actively think about things afterward. Certainly you can explore ways that you can improve. But don't harp on your mistakes. Everybody makes them. Experience and thoughtful analysis will continue to make you a better bargainer.

CHAPTER 2

THE SILENT
BARGAINING
QUIZ

Suppose that you are going to meet someone in New York City. You know the day and the time, but not the place. Where would you go?

No doubt this sounds pretty strange. Why in the world would you ever have to meet someone and not know where to go? Suppose there is more to the story. You received a call from the well-known, very rich, and eccentric Dr. Brown. She told you that she chose you and one other person to solve the following problem. Exactly two weeks from the day of her call you must meet this other person in New York City. She wouldn't identify this person except to say that he/she was another normal adult like you. If you chose the same place and met each other exactly at three o'clock, each of you would receive one million dollars.

If either of you tried to find out the other's identity, via newspaper ads or any other means, the deal would be off. You were also not allowed to have any assistance in solving the problem: Any evidence of colluding with anyone meant that you would forfeit your right to the prize. Each of the two of you had to solve the problem alone. That afternoon each of you would carry a large stuffed animal to the place you selected so that you could easily recognize each other. Dr. Brown suggested Bugs Bunny for you and Mickey Mouse for the other person. If you missed each other, or you were late, you wouldn't get anything. To claim your prize, the two of you, together, had to call her between three o'clock and three-ten that day. "That's it," she said, "and good luck!"

You knew from numerous magazine and newspaper stories that Dr. Brown had pulled outrageous stunts like this before. They were always well publicized since she always paid off. So now the task makes more sense. It's certainly unusual, but it also could be a dream come true. The only problem, of course, is where to go.

Right after Dr. Brown's call, when you realized that this deal was for real, you got very excited. A big adrenaline rush hit, and you were bursting with thoughts and energy and desire. After it dawned on you that your chances of winning were pretty low, though, you shifted from excitement to depression. With luck, these two phases passed quickly.

Then you could begin to think this puzzle through. A truly optimistic outlook on this weird deal is that you will always have a wonderful story to tell, even if you don't win. But wouldn't it be nice to solve it and win a million dollars?

Your task is deceptively simple. If you could somehow figure out who the other person was, you could call her and arrange where you would go. But after a little thinking, it becomes clear that there is no way for you to find out who this person might be. On top of that, Dr. Brown ruled out any attempts to do so.

You're also not allowed to go to New York early and carry a big Bugs Bunny with you wherever you go, hoping to see someone carrying Mickey Mouse and scanning crowds just like you. So this is not a solution either.

The problem boils down to figuring out exactly where the other person will go. Thus, you must try to think about how she is thinking. At the same time, you realize that she will be thinking about how you are thinking. You both could get caught up in a vicious cycle of wondering whether she is thinking that you are thinking what she is actually thinking—et cetera, et cetera. You can avoid all this by simply concentrating on trying to predict how she will think and where she will go. You hope that she does the same about you.

In a strange way, then, you will be bargaining with this unknown person without talking with her. That is not like normal bargaining since you can't communicate with each other. But you and the other person will both be acting strategically and interdependently. You will both be trying to figure out what the other is thinking and what the other might do. It's a lot like the preliminaries to a big negotiation. Thus, we can say that you are bargaining, even though you are not communicating.

How can you predict what the other person will be thinking when you know nothing about her? At first glance, you might think that you have nothing to go on. But that is not completely true. Almost everyone knows something about New York. That is a pretty safe assumption. But you ask yourself, "How much does this particular person know?" Since you won't be able to identify her ahead of time, you'll never be able to figure this out exactly; she won't be able to figure this out about you either.

You might assume that she is a lot like you and knows New York about as well as you do. That can't be entirely true—no one is just like you—but it does provide a way to begin. In fact, it's what people often do when they try to predict how other people feel about something. (When people muse about the possibility of opening a restaurant or a store, they almost automatically think that their customers will like the same things they do.)

So what do you know about places in New York City? What places come to mind first? When Thomas Schelling first presented this problem to his students at Yale University in the 1950s, more of them chose Grand Central Station than anywhere else—something of a surprise. The explanation, though, was fairly clear: Most of them traveled to New York by train. They arrived at Grand Central. If they thought they would be meeting someone like themselves, the train station was a perfect, central location to meet.

But these Yale students were a pretty select group. Your problem is tougher. Your partner could be anyone. If she is a baseball fan, she might choose Yankee Stadium. If she loves art, she might choose the Museum of Modern Art or the Metropolitan. If she has a business background, she might choose the New York Stock Exchange. But those are all places that depend on a set of interests that you won't be able to identify. Other places have more mass appeal, like Rockefeller Center, Times Square, the UN Building, the World Trade Center, and the Chrysler Building. There are two other places that really stand out: the Empire State Building and the Statue of Liberty. Let's assume that you narrow down the possibilities to these two. How would you choose between them?

You could go and investigate both places to see if one or the other offers a better location for finding a stranger carrying a Mickey Mouse doll. If you did, you would find that neither has much of an advantage over the other in helping you locate someone. Both are open enough to make it easy to spot some-one carrying Mickey. If she is there at the right time, and you are too, you won't miss each other.

So which should you choose?

Before I reveal what most people choose, it's time for a short quiz. This quiz is a series of questions that all have one thing in common with the New York City problem. The correct answer is the answer that almost everyone gives. So to do well, you have to think about how other people will answer these questions and answer them the same way. Thinking about the New York City problem should have been good preparation.

Remember: Don't necessarily answer the questions the way you normally would. Answer them the way that you think most other people have answered them—realizing, of course, that they were trying to answer as everyone else did, too. Good luck!

THE SILENT BARGAINING QUIZ

(Note: Many of these questions come from Thomas Schelling's book, *The Strategy of Conflict.*)

1. Heads or tails. Which do you choose?
2. Choose one of the following boxes:

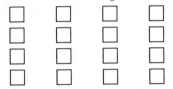

3. a. You are supposed to meet someone in Paris (not New York City). You know the day and the time, but not the place. Where would you go?

   b. The same question, but this time it's London.

4. A distinguished, attractive gentleman (who also looks wealthy) presents you with a proposition. He says that he is willing to pay everyone responding to this quiz a sum of money. If you and ninety-nine others all ask for the same amount of money independently, that's what he will pay each of you. If everyone doesn't come up with the same amount, everyone gets nothing.

   How much will it be?

5. The first ballot in a political election has been tabulated. These are the results:

Brown	15
Jones	28
Robinson	19
Smith	29
White	9

   Your interest in this election is purely political. You do not care who is elected as long as you vote for the winner. In the second ballot, who will you vote for?

6. Divide $100 into two piles. If everyone divides the $100 the same way, everyone will win $100.

7.   a. Sandy is in the market for a new (or used) car. She has been looking around for some time and has found just the car she would like to buy. It's the right color; it has the right options; it will suit her needs just fine. When she inquires about price, the sellers say that it's $10,650.

What will the final price of the car be—exactly?

b. Change the story slightly. Now Sandy is buying a used car for her daughter. It also fills the bill just fine. The selling price is quoted as $2,650.

What will the final price of the car be?

c. Same question as b, but now the price is $2,450. Again, what will the final price of the car be?

THE ANSWERS AND SOME EXPLANATIONS

For a long time, social scientists have based their studies of people on the belief that we all behave the way we do because we are affected by two forces: (1) our unique, individual characteristics and (2) the characteristics of the situation. A simpler way of saying this is that behavior is a function of the person and the environment.

Each of these quiz questions established an isolated situation. Some were familiar, like buying a car or voting for a political candidate. Others were less common, but none of them should have been very perplexing. Thus, everyone probably used some implicit rules to choose their answers. As we go through each question, I'll discuss some of these rules, which are often called schemas or scripts.

1.   When we toss a coin and someone chooses heads or tails, most people—in fact, a great majority—choose heads. When someone chooses tails, we take notice because it's fairly unusual.

Most people also choose heads on this quiz. They assume that people know how prevalent heads is called in actual coin flips, so they choose heads just as they would if we were flipping a coin. None of this is very surprising—except for the fact that everyone taking the quiz does *not* choose heads! About 10 percent of most groups choose tails. Choosing tails is not wrong when you're actually flipping a coin—it's just as likely as heads (if it's a fair coin). But choosing tails on this quiz *is* wrong, and people realize it quickly when everyone else's answers are revealed.

2. The most popular choice for North Americans and Europeans is the box in the upper left-hand corner. Other choices concentrate on the main diagonal, usually close to the top. Occasionally people choose boxes off the Main diagonal. When they are asked to explain why, they never seem to be able to come up with a good reason for their choice—unless they come from another culture. Israelis, for example, often choose the upper right-hand corner. This is probably because we see these boxes in the same way that we see words on a page. We read from the top down, from left to right. Hebrew is also read from the top down, but from right to left. Thus, the first box people see and choose corresponds to the first word they would read on a page, regardless of where it is. One thing is pretty clear, however; even with different cultures, corner answers are right and interior answers are wrong.

3. a. Where should we meet someone in Paris? The overwhelming choice is the Eiffel Tower. Everything else is a distant second. People also mention Notre Dame, the Left Bank (which is not very specific), and the Louvre.

b. In London, the choices are spread out more widely. The most frequent choice is Big Ben. Westminster Abbey, Trafalgar Square, and Buckingham Palace are also frequently mentioned.

I should note here that most of the responses I have tabulated for this quiz come from people enrolled in a variety of MBA and executive courses I have taught in the United States. The majority of my students are American, but many other cultures are also represented.

4. How much money would you like? Everyone does *not* say $1 million. Surprised? I was. Why would anyone say anything else? Many people say $100, a few less say $1,000, and even fewer ask for $10,000 or $100,000. Note that, except for very unusual cases (most often jokes), everyone's requests are in multiples of 10.

    When I vary this question by saying that *I* am the one making the offer, the estimates drop, but not for everyone. Many people still ask for $1 million. Some take the fact that I am a professor into account and list $5, $10, and $25—multiples of 5 rather than 10 and much lower amounts than before.

5. Whom did you vote for? Not too surprisingly, Smith is a consistent winner. Smith had the most votes the first time around and almost everyone votes for the top vote-getter on the second ballot. Jones, who had received almost as many votes as Smith (28 versus 29), always comes out a distant second. Almost no one else gets any votes at all. Most people have no difficulty adopting a strictly political position; a minority thinks that everyone will go for the underdog.

6. How people divide $100 into two piles also produces some surprising results; not everyone divides it into two $50 piles. Intuitively, this seems to be the easiest question in this quiz. The push to 50-50 is very strong and has been observed over and over again in many contexts (as we will see). Why anyone would choose anything else is beyond understanding—even the understanding of the people making those choices! Those few people who make different choices still propose divisions that are multiples of 10, for example, 60-40, 70-30, or 90-10. They have a terrible time explaining their choices.

7. a. You know nothing about Sandy or the used car market she is in. But you do know that she probably

wouldn't offer more than $10,650 for this car. You might also expect the sellers to (eventually) come down from their starting price. In the end, you might figure that they will settle somewhere between Sandy's first offer and the seller's first asking price.

Most people say that the final price will be $10,000. Other estimates range between $9,000 and $10,650. Many people claim that Sandy's first offer should be $10,000 and that she wouldn't go any higher than that.

b. When the starting price is $2,650, the dominant choice is $2,500—it's even more popular than $10,000 in the first version of the question. Some estimates fall between $2,500 and $2,650; a few come in below $2,500.

c. When the starting price is only $2,450, $2,000 is the most popular estimate, and it's almost as frequent as $2,500 in part b.

How did you do? Most people do quite well on this quiz. They get most of the answers correct. In fact, when you find out the correct answers, it becomes immediately obvious that they are right. Whether you were right or wrong, almost no one argues about the right answers. The most frequent answers within a single culture are obviously right; all others are obviously wrong. This is actually very surprising. On a quiz like this, where there are so many possibilities, unanimous agreement about the correct answers is remarkable.

The reason for all this agreement is actually pretty simple. The solutions to these questions are all *prominent:* They stand out; they're obvious; they're familiar. Prominent choices are often the first alternative we encounter (like heads or the upper left-hand corner). When they are numbers, they're round (like 50-50 or $1 million). Or they stick out—literally—because they're tall, like the Eiffel Tower or Big Ben.

Almost everyone gets at least one of these questions wrong. But now that the right answer is obvious, you might ask yourself why you didn't see it before. You may have suffered from what I call *the purple chicken problem.* Once someone says, *"Don't* think of a purple chicken," that's all you can think of. In the same way, people often fixate on the solution that has jumped into their mind. It's hard for them to see how any other answer is possible—if they can even think of another answer, since their purple chicken takes over their brain—until they hear that other answer and realize their mistake. When people make a non-prominent choice, their choice is prominent for them *at that time*. Only when they see that almost everyone else has chosen another answer do they realize their mistake. Then they can re-place the purple chicken with the right answer.

Each of these questions was like a mini-negotiation. Each had a prominent solution, which is one of the basic, underly-ing characteristics of many bargaining games. As we will see, bargainers may not realize it, but they often end up at a prominent solution—almost despite themselves. The situation or structure within each of the questions in the Silent Bar-gaining Quiz determines what's prominent. The same thing happens in many negotiations: An underlying structure makes one outcome more obvious and more reasonable than any of the other possibilities.

Different cultures can shift the structure of a bargaining game and, as a result, the right answer or the most reasonable outcome of a negotiation also shift. Take the Paris question as an example. When we discussed the New York problem, we narrowed down the locations to two, but that wasn't easy. The big difference between the Paris and New York versions of the question, and the reason that the Eiffel Tower is over-whelmingly prominent, is that most Americans know *less* about Paris than they do about New York. The Eiffel tower may be the only location that pops into the heads of people who don't know Paris. Not knowing much is actually an ad-vantage in this situation. People who know Paris well have a much harder time making their choice. They can generate so many alternatives to the Eiffel Tower that their chances of being right become quite slim.

People who know New York City well have the same prob-lem. If you know the city, your chances of picking the wrong answer increase. You might be swayed toward choosing the

World Trade Center or Times Square rather than the Empire State Building or the Statue of Liberty, which are more obvious choices to people who don't know the city. Thus, people who don't know New York are actually in a better position to solve this problem and win a million dollars. Not having information is not usually an advantage. As we will see later, more information is almost always much better than less.

The flip side of the concept of prominence, by the way, is that nonprominent places, times, or numbers make people take notice. Those who choose tails over heads, for example, get a little more attention for their choice. More important, some people use nonprominence very effectively. They make appointments at odd times, like eight minutes past two. It's much harder to forget or be late for an appointment at 2:08 than at 2:00. People who use this idea report that their meetings start much more punctually than they do at normal (prominent) meeting times.

AUTOMOBILE STRATEGIES

As we've mentioned, people never buy a car and tell their friends that they got a bad deal, even though most of us are far from experts. The way many people respond to the three car questions in the Silent Bargaining Quiz helps make this point clearly.

In the first car question, the starting price was $10,650. (Throughout this discussion, I assume that the car is worth something like this amount of money.) Prominence suggests that the car should sell for $10,000. Many people also think—correctly—that an average, interested buyer will start the bargaining by *offering* $10,000. If the first offer is going to be the final price, though, then the buyer's first offer must have been take-it-or-leave-it. But that is unusual. Instead, when sellers come down from their initial asking price—say, to $10,500—it then becomes the buyer's turn to make a concession. The norm for reciprocating concessions is very strong;

it is the definition of bargaining in good faith. If a deal is going to happen, then, people who start by offering $10,000 may end up paying more if they finally buy the car. Here we can see that the prominent solution to this item on the Silent Bargaining Quiz might *not* be the most likely outcome if this scenario were actually played out.

This bargaining process, however, exactly fits the plan of a smart, intuitive car seller. By setting the starting price at $10,650, she helped influence the buyer to start with a prominent offer, $10,000. After that, she can be sure of getting at least $10,000 for the car, and maybe more.

Some people who thought $10,000 would be the final selling price realized that the buyer had to start at less than $10,000. The important bargaining point here is that the buyer's first offer must set up $10,000 as the *final* price. Thus, to do well, potential buyers must resist the immediate force of prominence and avoid opening the bargaining at $10,000.

The different starting prices for the two less expensive cars make a tremendous difference in the prominence of the final price and the bargaining that is necessary to get there. By starting at $2,650, the sellers almost imply that they have a bottom price of $2,500. When the price drops $200 (to $2,450), the implied bottom line drops to $2,000.

The point here is clear: If at all possible, sellers should set the starting price just above an obviously prominent point. By doing so, they can implicitly encourage buyers to start their bidding at the prominent point and ensure a good final price. People are almost always compelled toward prominent solutions and, as a result, they may not even think of other possibilities.

In his original description of prominence, Schelling told a story that shows how important it can be. He described the predicament of two paratroopers who lost radio contact with one another. Finding each other in open country at night can be particularly difficult. If either or both of them got confused and couldn't locate their rendezvous point, they might never hook up. The locale, though, might still offer them an obvious solution. If they landed in an open field, a high point or a tree might provide the best place to meet. If they landed near a small town, the church steeple might identify a prominent meeting place. For everyone who found their rendezvous or didn't lose contact, such prominent points could be used as secondary meeting places where stragglers might be recovered. Discovering the prominent solution in this case might mean the difference between life and death.

COLLECTIVE BARGAINING

Prominence can also influence the process and outcomes of labor-management negotiations. In their landmark book on collective bargaining, *A Behavioral Theory of Labor Negotiations,* Richard Walton and Robert McKersie tell a story about the president of a small manufacturing company who was preparing for contract negotiations. The union had recently completed negotiations with other firms in the industry and each time had settled on the same wage increase of a dollar an hour. (I've inflated this pay raise to reflect economic inflation since the actual time of this story.) The company president wanted to avoid all of the wrangling and positioning and give-and-take that so often accompany labor-management negotiations. He met with his personnel officers and told them that he was going to truncate the bargaining process by offering the union the $1-an-hour wage increase right off the bat. He knew and the union knew that that would be the final outcome anyway. Why not just lay it out and get things finished?

His personnel officers tried to dissuade him, but he was vehement. When negotiations began, he used his opening statement to summarize the other agreements in the industry and suggested that they finish negotiations immediately and settle on the $1-an-hour wage increase. He said that this was management's first offer and its last offer and that they should just shake hands on the deal and go home.

Without knowing anything about the president and his bargaining strategies, we would expect that prominence would increase the chances of a $1-an-hour agreement. The number *1* is tremendously prominent—it's the first of all integers; it signifies being the best; and all the other firms in the industry had already agreed to it.

As it turned out, the company president should have listened to his personnel people. The union responded to his opening statement by saying that they would like to caucus and discuss management's opening offer. They came back from their caucus after a short discussion, thanked the company president for his opening offer, and talked about scheduling their next meeting so they could formulate an appropriate response. They emphasized the words "opening offer."

The negotiations took longer than usual, as the president tried to hang tough and hold to what he considered a thoroughly reasonable position. But the union's demands that the company bargain in good faith and reciprocate concessions (an extremely strong norm in collective bargaining) finally got management to yield. The agreement was much more favorable to the union than a dollar an hour.

THE NEW YORK CITY DILEMMA

We finally return to New York City and the problem of where to go. When it comes right down to it, what would you do? Would it be the Statue of Liberty or the Empire State Building? It's too bad that this problem doesn't have a straightforward prominent solution. It's not as easy as choosing heads in a coin flip, going to the Eiffel Tower in Paris, or dividing $100 into two piles of $50 each.

You *could* flip a coin to determine where you will go. But there are certainly more reasonable ways to decide. A little library research, for instance, might help. You might check the popular books and writings about New York City and count the number of times the Empire State Building and the Statue of Liberty are mentioned. Travel guides and encyclopedias would be useful sources. After doing your research, you could go to the place mentioned most, knowing that you had made the best choice you could (even if it was wrong). But, without the research, if you had to choose right now, where would you go?

People who answer this question as part of the Silent Bargaining Quiz choose the Empire State Building more than the Statue of Liberty. It may be that the fame of King Kong and Fay Wray still dominate our thinking about New York—as Al Capone dominates foreigners' first thoughts about Chicago. It may be its central location, in midtown Manhattan. Whatever the reason, it beats the Statue of Liberty. If the other person facing this problem should happen to be anything like my students, going to the Empire State Building would increase your chances of winning.

Also, if you *had* done some library research before you went, you might have discovered that the actual location of the Statue of Liberty is unclear. Some maps show it in New Jersey rather than New York. Indeed, Hudson County, New Jersey, claims it. On the other hand, Manhattan and New York County also claim it. Thus, you might ask yourself, if you went to the Statue of Liberty, would you really be in New York? It would be really sad to lose this contest on a technicality, which is one more reason for going to the Empire State Building.

THE POWER OF PROMINENCE

Sometimes bargaining outcomes are obvious, even before the bargaining begins. The bargainers themselves may not realize this. They're too busy trying to analyze the situation and find an advantage they can exploit. But outside observers can often see it and afterward, with the benefits of hindsight, the bargainers themselves may see it, too.

The moral of this chapter, then, is that prominence is a very important factor in bargaining. It underlies many negotiations, it can have a potent effect on the outcome of a negotiation, but it's not the sole determiner of what will happen. The traditions of collective bargaining, for instance, can override the strength of prominence, as they did when the company president tried to circumvent the normal bargaining process. If he had gone about the negotiations normally, they would almost certainly have reached the prominent $1-an-hour solution. It might have meant many bargaining sessions, some lasting throughout the night, and they might not have agreed until just before the deadline. In the end, however, it's a good bet they would have reached the prominent solution. Thus, although prominence is powerful, it pays to be careful and not assume that it will dominate everything else.

Prominence is not a singular concept: It's fuzzy and can come in any of several forms (first, tallest, etc.). But it does make sense. We recognize it immediately when we think of it. It pays to pay attention to it in negotiations.

The presence of a prominent solution is one of the most basic aspects of the structure of a bargaining game, whether the game is silent and without contact or more normal. Thus, *the structure of the game itself sometimes dictates the final outcome.* Even when it doesn't, prominence can limit the range of possible outcomes. When a prominent solution exists, it will be the most likely outcome. Thus, when you recognize the presence of prominent solutions and, more generally, the driving forces provided by the underlying structure of a bargaining game, you should work within that structure to your best advantage.

This advantage need not be one-sided. If you are in a negotiation and the other party does not see what should happen, you can still implement a strategy that moves both of you to the reasonable, prominent solution. Just as people taking our quiz realized the obviousness of the correct answer almost immediately, so too can uninformed, less experienced bargainers realize that, even though you were a more adept bargainer, the situation had a strong hand in determining the final outcome of your negotiation. And this outcome was what *should* have happened, given the structure of the game.

EMOTIONAL
DEVILS

One of the basic truths in bargaining is that emotions can spoil what might otherwise be a good negotiation. Letting emotions take over in the middle of a negotiation, or even before it begins, usually leads to a lousy outcome. When adrenaline is charging through your veins, it's hard to be calm, cool, and creative. You can't pay attention to the important dynamics of a negotiation. Instead, your focus gets centered on yourself and how you are feeling.

There are three main culprits here: nerves, anger, and the fear of losing face. They are all emotional devils. Although we generally accept that they can ruin a negotiation, researchers have done surprisingly little to document their impact.

Nerves lead people to focus more on how they might screw things up than on how they can do better. When some people go to buy a horse or a car, they're timid and embarrassed and try not to make fools of themselves. Their self-focus makes it impossible for them to concentrate on the issue at hand and bargain well.

With anger, on the other hand, people often can't see past the fact that the individuals they are dealing with are *totally awful*—so bad, in fact, that all they can do is vent their frustrations and be done with them. Blind rage fuels blind, emotional action. Negotiations can even go beyond verbal interaction and turn into physical violence. This rarely endears one bargainer to another.

On other occasions—possibly most situations where we get angry—we don't express it. In our highly civilized, regulated society, making a scene and screaming at someone in public is totally inappropriate. Thus, when we do get angry, we often bottle it up—so it can stew and fester and breed even more antagonism. Some people get angry easily and lose their anger just as rapidly. But for others, anger is like rust—it may lie dormant, but it never sleeps. When it finally comes out, it can really explode. The poor recipient may have little or no forewarning that this explosion is coming, and no way of knowing why we are so angry.

Getting a negotiation back on a constructive track is extremely difficult after an angry outburst. The other person may not even remember the original incident, even if you can cool down enough to describe it. If they want to make amends, you may find it difficult to forget either the original incident or the accumulated anger that you have harbored ever since.

Anger can have a positive side in negotiations. The old saying that "the squeaky wheel gets the grease" is often true. When you have purchased something that doesn't work, for example, it usually pays to demand satisfaction (within reason). Getting angry at an uninformed sales clerk may not help them help you, but it may bring a supervisor with some discretion onto the scene. It's important to note that the anger we are talking about here is anger that you keep under control. Breaking a store's furniture and smashing its windows is not a good bargaining tactic. But being insistent and possibly raising your voice after friendly requests haven't worked can be very effective.

Anger can also be manipulated to have a positive effect. Richard Walton and Robert McKersie's book on collective bargaining contains another story that's relevant here. Most head negotiators meet with each other privately outside the bargaining room to discuss their expectations. During negotiations, they not only have to deal with each other's demands, but they must also deal with the demands of their own constituents. They might agree on a tremendous contract, but if the labor negotiator can't convince the union membership or the management negotiator can't convince the company's board of directors to approve it, there will be no agreement.

Thus, even when things should be easy—when a labor-management contract has an obvious, prominent solution and both sides respect each other and get along—both sides still have to act as if they are bargaining hard. Their constituents must believe that they didn't accomplish anything easily. Both head negotiators must impress their constituents that they couldn't have bargained harder.

With this in mind, one head negotiator may inform the other privately that, in their next meeting, he is going to get very upset—he's going to rant and rave and storm out, and he's not going to bring his side back to the table for several days. The two chief negotiators will be the only people to know this in advance. Everyone else, including the members of both negotiating teams, may wonder what's up. A successful acting job like this can awaken both sides and make them believe that their representatives are working extremely hard to get everything they can. In some situations, it makes the confirmation of a final agreement easier.

A similar scenario is played out (frequently?) in major league baseball games. Leo Durocher, who managed the Brooklyn Dodgers, the New York Giants, and the Chicago Cubs, gave the appearance of being a tempestuous leader. It's said that what sometimes looked like one of his angry eruptions at the umpires was actually a well-orchestrated act. Durocher would storm out of the dugout, hollering and yelling, but this is what he may actually have been saying: "I know you're trying to do your job! I know you're not blind! But I have to fire up my team and get them motivated! So I'm going to kick some dirt on your shoes. And you should kick some on mine! I'll holler a little more with my mouth wide open and my nose within inches of yours! Then you will throw me out of the game! Thanks!"

These two examples—a manager and a head negotiator, both looking angry to create an effect—are exceptions to the general rule. Anger usually interferes with effective negotiating.

I should probably refine that to say that *uncontrolled* anger usually interferes with effective negotiating. To put it simply, how can two really angry people cooperate with each other?

FEAR OF LOSING FACE

The fear of losing face involves both fear and pride. The two compound themselves to become the third emotional devil in bargaining. The loss of face is extremely important in Asian cultures, where it can even be accompanied by the voluntary loss of life. In Japan, for instance, once you lose face, your dishonor may be too much to live with. Even in Western cultures, the effects are both short-term and long-term: Currently humiliation may disappear but a seriously damaged reputation may be difficult to eradicate.

Saving face comes into play when a negotiator takes a public stand and then has to back down. The public may include large audiences and international media or just one person—the person he is bargaining with. The fear of backing down and losing face is particularly disruptive when a concession can help achieve a particularly beneficial agreement. Take, for instance, a labor negotiator who makes a public statement that the union will not accept anything less than a 10 percent wage increase. To save face, he might reject an agreement that gives the union tremendous medical and fringe benefits but only a 9-percent raise. Similarly, political candidates who campaign with pledges of no new taxes may contribute to economic chaos after their election by refusing to increase taxes that are obviously necessary.

Making sure that your opponent has room to back down gracefully, without losing face, can be an essential element in negotiations, especially when you have the upper hand. The Cuban missile crisis is a perfect example. In October 1962, intelligence sources revealed that the USSR had begun installing a missile base in Cuba—much too close to the coast of Florida to be tolerated by the United States. President John F. Kennedy confronted the Russians and demanded that they immediately remove the missiles. Throughout the bargaining that followed, however, he carefully preserved ways for Nikita Khrushchev to concede gracefully. In particular, Kennedy ignored the Russians' strongest statements, and predicated all of his actions on Khrushchev's more conciliatory messages. By doing so, he preserved Khrushchev's opportunity to concede. Khrushchev finally did back down, and the United States and the Soviet Union were able to avoid a particularly dangerous game that threatened world peace.

THE BLIND PARTNERSHIP GAME

As the old saying goes, "Fool me once, shame on you; fool me twice, shame on me." The Blind Partnership Game offers people the chance to be fooled twice, since they play it repeatedly. The game also includes the possibility for all three emotional devils: Nervousness afflicts some people when they play this game for the first time; anger follows negotiations when people disagree about whether someone's tactics were unethical or simply strategic; and people lose face when they are fooled and should have known better.

Here are the rules of the game:

- Groups of almost any size can play.
- Anyone can bargain with any other individual bargainer.
- Everyone is randomly given a number that represents her wealth.
- By itself each person's number is useless—it provides no value until two people combine their numbers.
- Then their joint wealth is real and they can share its benefits.
- They must negotiate how they will split up their total wealth *before* they know for sure what their partner's

number is; they can say what their number is, but they can't physically show their number to anyone. In other words, they can't *prove* that they're telling the truth when they say what their number is.

Everyone needs a partner. Any pair of people can divide the total of their resources any way they want, just as in a normal partnership. Unlike a normal partnership, however, they negotiate how they will split up their total wealth before they know their partner's number.

The strange part of this game is that no one knows how good her own number really is. Some people start with high numbers and some with low—but no one knows what is low and what is high. All anyone knows for sure is her own number, the rules of the game, and that finishing with more is clearly better than finishing with less. Most people understand that it pays to form a partnership with someone who has a high number. If no one reveals the value of her number, though, how can you bargain effectively? This question makes some bargainers very nervous.

I have often had groups of about forty people play this game. People negotiate as they tour the room to see who will offer them how much. They can reach any agreement they like as long as they follow the rules. With an even number of people negotiating, no one hurries very much—someone will always be available as a partner. With an odd number of people, however, negotiations are more urgent since no one wants to be the person left out.

Let's say that you are playing the Blind Partnership Game and that your number is 500. You know that you can say anything you want to anyone; you must find a partner and agree how to split the total of your two numbers. You know that you can reveal the value of your number, but you don't know whether that would be a good idea.

The primary issue for you is whether 500 is a low number or a high number. If it's high, and you are an attractive, wealthy partner, you can relax a bit and try to make sure that you walk away with at least 500. But if 500 is actually a low number, you'll need to find someone with a better number if you want to improve your outcome. The problem is, if you don't even know whether your number is high or low, how will you know if someone else's number is high or low?

THE PLAY IN GAME ONE

Anything and everything happens when people play this game for the first time. Most agreements are 50-50 or keep-your-own; there are several more complicated arrangements, too. Some players reveal their numbers; most don't. When people do reveal their numbers, most tell the truth. As a result, some people find out what's high and what's low.

Finding that you have a high number is very helpful. You can then turn your attention to preserving your wealth. Finding that you have a low number, however, is not so good. It still helps you strategically, but now other people may also know that you are not such a great partner. That reduces your pool of potential partners. You need to adjust your strategy to look for a high number who does not realize his good fortune. Some people with low numbers do find high numbers and split 50-50. They have done very well in a difficult position. But with this first play, it's sometimes hard to tell whether they were good or lucky. (They always claim they were good.)

Some low-high pairs decide to keep their own numbers, which is a very good deal for the high numbers. Any time a high-numbered player reaches an agreement with a low-numbered player, there is a good chance the high-numbered player will lose something. Quite a few high-numbered players also find high-numbered players. Most of them bargain effectively and keep their own number. Others split 50-50—and are very lucky. If they had been dealing with a low-numbered player instead, they would have been stung. Finally, several low-numbered pairs form and are more likely to split 50-50 than to keep their own number. Either way, they still finish with a low total.

For this first play of the game, I assign numbers from 20 to 35 and 490 to 505. Thus, 500 is a very good number. The low numbers in this distribution are so low that people who have them usually get some idea that they are stuck with little wealth. People with high numbers, on the other hand, are usually less confident: They can't be sure that no one has a much higher number. They do get a good idea that their number is high, however, if they hear anyone revealing a low number. That is why revealing your number can be a very bad strategy if your number is low—you give others, possibly many others, information that makes them avoid you as a partner.

THE TWO STRATEGIES

If everyone revealed their numbers, everyone would agree on the same strategy: Keep your own. Both people would know whose number was higher, so any scheme other than keep-your-own would cost the higher-numbered player. They're not likely to agree to that, so keep-your-own becomes a dominant outcome. (Occasionally, people are willing to give some of their wealth away, but that is unusual. As we will see, true altruists are rare.)

When people are aware of their number's value, or have guessed the value of other people's numbers, there are two basic strategies in the Blind Partnership Game: *split 50-50* and *keep your own*. For a low number, splitting 50-50 is an excellent strategy—*if* you connect with someone whose number is higher than yours. Other more complicated schemes might also help if you have a low number, but the 50-50 strategy is simplest and most prevalent.

Keeping your own is an excellent strategy if you have a high number. That way you don't lose what you have and you do well. You won't gain anything, so it's not a case of the rich getting richer. But you will preserve your wealth in a game where the risks of losing some of it far outweigh your opportunities to increase it.

The two strategies, 50-50 and keep-your-own, are pretty straightforward. The difficulty of knowing whether you have a low or a high number, however, doesn't disappear. Some people will try probes like, "What's your number?" or "Do you think you have a high number?" And others will avoid a direct answer, saying "Maybe" or "I *think* I have a high number." A second play of the game, with different numbers, provides more clues.

THE SECOND ROUND OF PLAY

This second game is conducted just like the first—same people, same rules—except everyone now has a new number. People have seen the first play of the game; they've had a chance to discuss what happened; they know the two basic strategies and when and why they work.

Everyone is now more attentive than last time; everyone is trying to hear what everyone else is saying and see what everyone else is doing. You (and everyone else) are on the lookout for the smallest indication that your number is low or high.

Everyone was just getting the hang of things in the first game. Now, it's time to pay more attention to people's subtle actions and reactions. In particular, nonverbal cues may signal something about the value of their number or yours. Good poker players pay a lot of attention to nonverbals. The idea is the same here. In fact, if you played many times, you would find that your blindness in this game would quickly disappear; you would become quite adept at learning the value of your number and other people's.

How can nonverbals help? If players grimace when they first look at their number, you can guess that it's probably low. If they react with a big smile, you might bet their number is high. Keeping your face unexpressive—a poker face—can be very valuable if you have a low number. If you have a high number, though, you might display your good fortune by smiling—it could help you find another high-numbered player quickly.

Let's assume that your number this time is 498. For the first game, this was a high number. Is it now? As you wander about, talking and trying to figure out what your best strategy should be, you find that several people approach you with 50-50 offers. It happens quite a bit. Most of these folks seem to be in a hurry to know whether you are interested. When you're not, they rush off in search of someone else. The repetitions of this scene make you think that your number is high again. You notice that someone else is turning away the same people that you are. You stroll up to her and ask if she thinks she has a high number. She says she's pretty sure she does, but she's not positive. You take a risk and say, "Is it around five hundred?" She smiles and says that that's pretty close. Then she offers to join you as a partner, with each of you keeping your own number. You agree.

By this time you are convinced that you have a high number. But you're not totally sure and you're worried that you somehow screwed things up. All this flashes through your mind instantaneously. You've already made your decision but you are briefly panic-stricken: What if your number is actually low? You turn to your partner so that you can reveal your numbers; you're holding your breath. Her number is 505. Whew! What relief. Your number was close to hers, which makes you more confident that you also have a high number. You must wait until everyone is finished to be sure, but you now only have a slight nervous feeling. Even if your number is low, you realize that your partner made the same mistake you did—you won't be the only one to have made the mistake.

It turns out that you didn't need to be nervous. Everyone knows that the keep-your-own strategy is good for high numbers and 50-50 is good for low numbers. By taking that a step further, it's also clear that someone offering 50-50 probably doesn't have a high number; if she did, she could lose a lot if she ran into someone with a low number. Alternatively, it makes little sense for someone with a low number to offer a keep-your-own agreement. By doing so, she sacrifices any chance she had to improve her outcome. Thus, keep-your-own is a *signal* that players think they have a high number; 50-50 is a signal that they think their number is low. So all those 50-50 offers were probably from people with low numbers. By waiting for a keep-your-own offer, you were in good shape to do well and preserve your wealth.

Even during this second game, someone almost always loses some of the advantage of her high number by agreeing with a low-numbered person for a 50-50 split. Sometimes these outcomes are accompanied by anger and an accusation that the low-numbered player said she had a high number. Is this accusation fair? On the one hand, it certainly could be. This game provides people with the opportunity to misrepresent their numbers, and deliberate falsehoods are almost always unethical. On the other hand, though, people have bargained poorly when they are lured into a 50-50 split when they know they have a high number and they understand the two basic strategies. Any high-numbered player can ensure a good outcome by simply sticking to keep-your-own. Splitting 50-50 is an unnecessary risk that may be driven by greed. Some of this anger, then, should be self-directed.

These sad outcomes highlight an important lesson in this game: It's not always what you've got and what the other person has that is important. Instead, it's what you *think* you've got and what you *think* the other person has. This can be true in poker, business, war, and any number of other bargaining games.

With experience, people learn to quickly discover whether they have a low or a high number. No one can ever be completely sure, of course, but confidence in detecting who has what kind of number increases dramatically with experience. In fact, confidence usually outdistances accuracy: Experience often makes people overconfident. They become more prone to misreading subtle cues and jumping to the wrong conclusions. It's important, then, whenever you're negotiating, to confirm, if you can, what you think you are sure of before you act.

STRATEGIES

Let's suppose that you could watch everyone in the Blind Partnership Game carefully (as Yogi Berra once said, "You can observe a lot by watching") and tell whether they had a high or low number quite accurately. Like the men who worked carnival sideshows by guessing your age or your weight with amazing accuracy, you could guess people's numbers. How would that help you in the game? If you had a high number, it would make things very easy. You would just find someone else with a high number and keep your own. But what would you do if you had a low number? How would you get away from the 50-50 strategy?

Knowing everyone's number won't help much unless you can impress someone with a high number that you too have a high number—*and* get her to agree to a 50-50 split. The *fait accompli* strategy sometimes works here: With a smirk on your face you approach someone with a high number and say, "So it looks like you have a high number, too." If she concurs, you can suggest that, although the two of you can't win or lose much by splitting 50-50, it would be more fun than keeping your own. If she agrees, you have used your knowledge that she has a high number, deceptively but effectively. Afterward, if she takes offense at your implying you had a high number, you have several defenses, the most salient being that both of you were negotiating and knew you were negotiating. (More on the ethics of the *fait accompli* tactic in Chapter 14.)

If you know everyone's numbers and you have the only high number left, you could be in trouble. You must stick to your guns and not settle for anything less than keeping your own—unless time is about to run out. Then you must hope a low-numbered player flinches—or flinch yourself before you lose it all.

It's rare for anyone to ever know everyone's number. More often, you may have a hunch that yours is a high number, and you may have hunches that several other people also have high numbers. It's almost like an old poker game that is played mostly for laughs. Everyone gets one card and is not allowed to look at it. Instead, when the dealer counts three, everyone holds their card on their forehead so that everyone else can see it. To win, you must bet on the only card you can't see—your own. Just as in the Blind Partnership Game, one of the keys is to find out what your own value is.

People don't normally take advantage of everyone else's nonverbals in this game. Rather than looking at how people look at them and their card, people tend to look first at everyone else's cards. Other people's cards do carry information. If someone has the ace of spades, you would have to induce her to drop out of the bidding if you wanted to have a chance at winning. But the information value of others' cards won't go away. Their nonverbals will. Thus, by seeing several people's eyes open wide when they see your card, you can get an idea that you have a good card. If people don't pause, but move past your card quickly, you can guess that your card is probably not so hot. People's immediate nonverbal reactions are usually the most revealing. But even if you carefully attended to everyone's early nonverbals, you would still be stuck with the uncertainty that almost always goes with nonverbal communication.

NONVERBAL BEHAVIOR

When we interact with someone face-to-face, whether to negotiate or for some other reason, our connection is more than verbal. Nonverbal communication adds an essential, complicating dimension to our interactions. Researchers have done extensive studies of how we communicate nonverbally.

Verbal communication is restricted to the actual words we use, whether they are spoken or written. Nonverbal communication includes everything else, including our intonation, gestures, posture, facial expressions, and body movements. Nonverbal communication can't be written down.

When verbal and nonverbal communication are consistent, the message is strong and clear. When someone says, "I love you," and his nonverbals reinforce the words, he sends a powerful message. When verbals and nonverbals are *not* consistent, however, the nonverbals win. Think of the same *nonverbal* cues from the "I love you" message and, keeping everything exactly the same—especially the vocals—change the words from "I love you" to "I hate you." What is the message now? The nonverbals are overwhelmingly positive; the tone is warm and inviting; the word "hate" is so out of place that it can't have its normal meaning. For most people, this new message is even stronger, and more positive, than "I love you."

Nonverbals can dominate a verbal message and totally

change its meaning—even though we don't often attend to them carefully. But, unlike verbal communication, which is almost unlimited, nonverbals are limited to *emotional* messages. They also can be difficult to interpret.

Before we go further, let me sound a strong word of warning. Although much of what I am about to discuss might imply that a good listener/observer can easily decipher how people feel from the way they express themselves nonverbally, that is definitely not the case. Although nonverbals can suggest how people are feeling, the cues are almost never perfectly clear. Thus, we should interpret nonverbal messages very cautiously.

Nonverbals are obviously important in bargaining. Some researchers describe nonverbal cues as a way that people inadvertently "leak" their feelings. To go to an extreme, let's say that you were at an antique fair; you saw something you liked, but you didn't want to appear too interested. You didn't want to give yourself away for fear that you wouldn't be able to negotiate a good price. But if sweat was pouring down the sides of your shirt or blouse, the seller would realize how interested you really were. Your perspiration would be *leaking* the fact that you were nervous and very interested.

Another example comes from the folklore of bargaining. Japanese jewelers supposedly pay close attention to the pupils of a customer's eyes. When your eyes dilate, it usually indicates that you are intrigued by what you see. When jewelers detect this nonverbal, emotional leak, they drive a much harder bargain.

The most commonly understood nonverbal behavior is eye contact. Everyone knows that making eye contact can help you appear credible and trustworthy. Someone who looks away and avoids eye contact is considered sneaky or devious.

Since eye contact is so well known, its positive message is rarely strong. Its negative side, however, can be very important. In my one and only formal job interview, I met with each of the seven faculty members in the organizational behavior group at the University of Illinois. Each interview lasted about forty-five minutes. When I met Gene, one of the younger faculty members, he never looked me in the eye. Here I was, the nervous job candidate, dutifully trying to establish eye contact, and he never once looked at me. Instead, he looked over my shoulder, at the carpet, at the ceiling. I really wondered what I had done wrong.

Afterward, he and Bill, another faculty member, took me to lunch. As the three of us walked through the center of campus, it was obvious that Gene and Bill were good friends. They had a lot to talk about and were obviously fairly close. As we ate, I noticed that Gene never looked Bill in the eye. What a relief! Gene's lack of eye contact had nothing to do with me or my behavior; he just didn't establish eye contact with anyone.

In negotiations, if you are bargaining with someone who does not look you in the eye, you might wonder, Is this person trying to hide something? Will she do what she says she'll do? What's the problem with this deal? Or is she just nervous? A *lack* of eye contact tells you more than its presence, but its message is still not perfectly clear. In addition, as the story about Gene and Bill testifies, everyone has a different nonverbal style. What might signify intimacy with one person may not signify anything at all with another.

It is particularly revealing when someone establishes eye contact comfortably most of the time, but then doesn't when he or she is bargaining with you. It is an obvious clue that something is amiss; it signals the need to be cautious and vigilant. Knowing a person's typical nonverbals and then seeing a departure from what they do normally is an important clue in negotiations. Thus, someone who rarely looks people in the eye, and then all of a sudden does, may be working very hard—too hard—to make a good impression. Similarly, the standoffish colleague who starts exuding inordinate charm should be easily recognized as someone trying to manipulate a situation for his own ends.

Nonverbals are not consistent, though, across different cultures. In America, for instance, we stand fairly far apart when we interact with people, even with friends. Getting closer than two feet is reserved for people who are intimate. In Turkey, however, people demand much less personal space. Even strangers stand close to each other when they speak. Thus, when

Americans visit Turkey for the first time, they think that the Turkish are overly forward and aggressive. When Turks visit North America, they think that everyone is distant and cold.

Other variations in personal space are also important. Women tend to sit next to people they like; men tend to sit across from people they like. Two social psychologists, Jeff Fisher and Donn Byrne, studied how students responded to someone who "invaded" their table in the library. They had a stranger sit near someone who was working alone. When they questioned people about these short, five-minute invasions, women reacted negatively and felt more crowded when the stranger sat next to them; men reacted negatively and felt more crowded when the stranger sat directly across from them. People also used their coats and other books to erect environmental barriers around their positions! Women tended to block the adjacent seat; men tended to block the seat across from them. Evolution can explain part of these findings: Men sit opposite each other, in full view, just in case one or the other should get aggressive and start to fight.

Other gender differences in nonverbal cues seem to be related. When two men are angry at each other, you can see them clench their teeth, exercising the muscles at the back of their jaws; other angry pairs (female-female and female-male) don't react this way as often.

Judith Hall, a social psychologist who has conducted a great deal of research on gender and nonverbal behavior, has found several notable differences in men's and women's nonverbal actions. Women are generally better at processing nonverbal cues; they recognize faces better; they gaze at and get closer to other people more; and they touch other people more than men do. They express their emotions more; they smile more; they are gazed at more; and people get closer to women than they do to men. It has been clear for a long time that men and women are different; their nonverbals may be one important aspect of their differences, and something worth keeping in mind when you negotiate. We shouldn't expect men and women to negotiate in exactly the same ways, and we shouldn't necessarily react differently when they don't.

When you meet a stranger, you may shake hands, but no other form of touching is normal, certainly not right away. Some people, however, touch the people they interact with frequently. Touch is an extreme form of personal space invasion. Everyone has met someone who is touchy, who tends to touch your arm or your shoulder soon after you meet. Usually, such people do this with everyone, just as my colleague Gene rarely looks anyone in the eye. When we realize that they are "touchers" and that we are nothing special, we no longer have to worry about what's going on: They aren't touching us because we have any special qualities. But touchers do make many people quite uncomfortable.

Touch is an obvious way to make a closer personal tie in negotiations. When someone is close to an important sale or a new business deal or a warmer interpersonal relationship, she may touch you on the forearm. That can be a calculated use of nonverbal behaviors, or it may simply indicate that this person is a "toucher." When sexual tension already exists between the people involved, a light touch can break the ice of an initial contact very rapidly. It increases intimacy and conveys that the other person is comfortable with you or wants you to be comfortable with her. It doesn't necessarily lead to intense intimacy, but it speeds up the process of establishing closeness in a relationship. A cynical interpretation of such behavior, of course, suggests that negotiators do this to help themselves rather than to convey how they feel—whether the bargaining is over a business deal or a possible romance.

Other gestures also imply positive and negative reactions, sometimes immediately. Smiling and leaning forward both show a favorable attitude. Leaning back, crossing your arms, and fidgeting in your seat are all negative signals, indicating boredom, lack of interest, or tension. Smiling is another nonverbal that people are quite conscious of. As a result, smiles can be manipulated more easily and, sadly, have become less meaningful than they would otherwise be. Paul Ekman, author of *Telling Lies,* says that smiles are "the mask most frequently employed."

A more expressive but (necessarily) less frequent positive signal is a wink. Winking is *the* nonverbal cue that loses its impact quickest when it is overused. People who wink too much should be accused of a social misdemeanor! Winks are special. People should save them for special occasions.

Leaning forward, another positive cue, has an additional, useful property: You can manipulate your physical position to lean forward and, as a result, increase your interest in what's happening. Instead of simply reacting nonverbally, without realizing what you are conveying, it's possible to consciously sit on the edge of your chair and, almost magically, feel as if you're more interested in what's going on.

A friend uses this technique fairly frequently. He has only two speeds: off and on. If he must sit still doing nothing for any length of time, he automatically switches to off and begins to fall asleep. That can be particularly embarrassing, for instance, if he is team-teaching a class and his partner is lecturing. When the class sees him sleeping, he detracts considerably from their appreciation of the material! His coteacher is not very appreciative either. He has learned, however, that he can perk himself up by consciously moving to the edge of his chair and leaning forward. By actively manipulating his own nonverbals, he can reverse the normal chain of events and stimulate the emotional feelings that usually precede the nonverbal reaction. That is particularly helpful during meetings with influential but boring speakers. By leaning forward and using only the edge of his seat, not only does he keep himself awake, but he also indicates to the speaker that he's interested.

If someone leans back and crosses her arms at something you've suggested in a negotiation, you can guess that she's not too excited about what you've been saying. When she leans forward, on the other hand, and seems eager to hear your every word, your confidence may grow.

Therapists have learned that nonverbals can help them relate more closely to their clients. By mimicking their clients' nonverbals, therapists can get a better appreciation of how they're feeling. A direct transfer of this idea to bargaining should be effective in much the same way.

A few more nonverbals are also important. A friend told me once that people who are discussing things that make them tense often stroke their index fingers across the bottom of their noses. She was uncanny at spotting people doing this. (I sometimes think that she consciously raised sensitive issues just to see whether she could provoke this response.) Lie detector tests are based on similar principles: When people lie, their tension usually manifests itself nonverbally. Arabs in the twelfth century made a similar use of nonverbals in a primitive version of the lie detector test: They judged a person's guilt by whether he could swallow a large mouthful of rice, without water. If a suspect couldn't generate enough saliva to get it down, he was obviously guilty.

Current findings indicate that when we are faced with someone who is lying, we can sometimes detect the lies, but it's not easy. As Paul Ekman put it: "Most liars can fool most people most of the time." Two factors, however, lead to successful detection: (1) Most people are poor liars, and (2) even though any one of us may not detect liars very often, as a society we are quite good at catching them. A lie might be successful in the short term with a small set of people, but it is usually detected sometime—and the costs of being caught can be tremendous, much worse than losing face.

Ekman identified four nonverbals as indicators of a lie: slips of the tongue; emotional tirades and outbursts; emblematic slips, where someone inadvertently displays an obvious nonverbal cue; and microexpressions, clear, one-quarter-of-a-second-long flashes of obvious emotions. None of the four are easily detected or frequently displayed. Other research, however, suggests that liars are most often tripped up not by their nonverbals, but by what they say.

CONCLUSIONS

I started this chapter with a discussion of emotions and argued that nerves, anger, and saving face are three emotions that can interfere with effective bargaining. We moved from there to the Blind Partnership Game, which was about knowing your own value—as you see it—and the value others have for you. People are often nervous before they play this game. They get angry when they feel that they've been swindled. And they lose face when they do badly a second time. Once they have played the game a couple of times, however, most residual nervousness disappears. Instead, people can direct their attention to others' strategies and the signals embedded within them, and to the nonverbals that people may leak. Experience provides us with the opportunity to be less nervous and, as a result, more effective when we bargain.

The lessons in the Blind Partnership Game are relevant in many contexts. Partnerships of all kinds are common arrangements that provide benefits to both parties. The optimal partnership is one in which each party can provide the other with great benefits while they themselves incur few costs. At the outset of a partnership, whether it is in business or romance or any other endeavor, there is always uncertainty, sometimes about your partner, sometimes about yourself. Are you as valuable to this partnership as you think you are? Is your partner as valuable as you think? These questions and the issues they generate are nicely reflected in the Blind Partnership Game.

Finally, we talked about the value of paying attention to nonverbals. They can be very revealing. Are they "the window to a person's soul"? Nonverbals are not that clear, but they are important cues to recognize in negotiations.

Knowing a person's normal nonverbals, and then seeing something that's not consistent, can provide an important signal. Those are exactly the times when your opponent may be getting ready to cook your goose, and when you should react.

CHAPTER 4

DILEMMAS, DILEMMAS

Once upon a time two burglars were caught by the police. They were escorted to separate jail cells so they couldn't connive. They knew the jig was up; they were headed back to jail for at least two years for parole violations. The police, however, had a deal: If one confessed to the burglary and the other didn't, the confessor could go free. The police didn't care which one confessed; any confession would save the police from admitting that they didn't have good evidence. The downside of the deal was that the burglar who didn't confess would get ten years hard time: "If your partner confesses and you keep quiet, *you* will go away for a long time and he will go free." The police also admitted—when pressed—that, if both burglars confessed, they would both be convicted of burglary. If that happened, the police assured them, they would put in a good word for them with the judge since they had been cooperative.

Each burglar faced four possible outcomes:

	He Keeps Quiet	He Confesses
I Keep Quiet	We each get two years.	He goes free; I get ten years.
I Confess	I go free; he gets ten years.	We each get about eight years.

If you were one of the burglars, what would you do? (This is not to suggest that you would ever actually be in this situation. Instead, as we will see, this story highlights the dilemma of cooperating or competing, even with a partner.)

First, you might consider what your partner will do. Let's say he decides to keep quiet. If you keep quiet, too, you get two years; if you confess, you go free. Thus, it's better for you to confess when your partner keeps quiet—you do two years less in jail.

But what if he confesses? Now if you keep quiet, you get ten years; if you confess, you get eight years. Thus, if he confesses, it's also better for you (by two years) to confess. Regardless of what he does, you avoid two years in jail by confessing.

It sounds like you should confess. The hitch—a big hitch—is that if he figures things out the same way, he's going to confess—just like you—and you will both get eight years, even though you both could have kept quiet and only gotten two years each.

This situation is called the prisoner's dilemma. The story was first told by economist A. W. Tucker in 1950. The police have probably known this game for a long time. So have criminals. It's just one version of a simple but compelling bargaining game. Another version, closer to home, is the Gas Station Game.

THE GAS STATION GAME

Now imagine a different situation, one that executive and student groups have frequently enacted. You and your partners own a neighborhood gasoline station. It is lucrative enough that you can hire people to handle the everyday business at the station. You and your partners merely have to act as supervisors. Not a bad deal. It is a franchise station, though, so you don't have a completely free hand in running things. At the same time, you and your partners make most of the major decisions.

Your nearest competitor is a station right across the street. Your station and theirs get most of the business in the area. Some people in the neighborhood are very loyal to you and your station; they only buy your gasoline and they depend on your mechanics to repair their cars. They have almost no regard for prices or other changes in the environment. They are wonderful, true-blue customers.

Most people in the neighborhood, however, are price-conscious; they always go to the station that is selling for less. As a result, both you and the other station make sure to display your prices clearly. You always notice each other's prices. Most of the time, your prices are exactly the same.

They are a franchise station, too. That means that you are both limited in how quickly you can change prices. If you want to cut prices (to get more business), you must first get the approval of your parent company. The same is true for your competitor. As it happens, the company bureaucracy is so slow that you are both stuck with a price for at least a week before you can change it.

If one station makes a change and sells for a lower price, and the other doesn't, the station with the lower price gets a lot more business. Whoever's price is higher always responds by also reducing their price, but it takes them a week to get approval. In the meantime, many customers go to the lower-priced station.

You and the owners of the other station are aware of these delays. You also know that either of you can make a killing—for a short time—if you cut your price and the other station doesn't. But cutting your price can be risky. It's almost like a preemptive nuclear strike—well, not quite.

The profits might look something like this: If both stations keep identical prices, each of you will make about $1,200 profit per week. If you cut your price and the other station doesn't, your profits will go up to $1,600 (because of increased sales), and they will only make $400. (If we assume relatively constant sales in the neighborhood, the total of the two stations' profits goes down, since one station has cut their price and, therefore, their profit margin.) The opposite is also true: If they cut their price and you don't, their profits will be $1,600 and you will only earn $400. If both of you happen to cut your prices at the same time, you'll each make only $800; all of your customers will be happy with the lower prices but they will choose between the two stations indiscriminately, and you and the other station will both earn less since you've cut your prices.

Both you and the other station realize the folly of cutting prices (this is an assumption that is not always true, as we will see later), so that if anyone cuts their price for a short time, you will both raise prices soon afterward to regain lost profits. The temptation to cut your price for a short-term gain, however, is always there.

It's a lot like major league sports these days: The owners know that they will profit less when they grant huge salaries to their star players. But they also know that they will lose business if they lose their best players to other, higher-paying teams.

In the Gas Station Game, you and the other station repeatedly face the following profit possibilities:

		They Choose to			
		Keep Constant		Cut Prices	
You	Keep Constant	$1,200	$1,200	$400	$1,600
Choose					
to	Cut Prices	$1,600	$400	$800	$800

The first number in each pair refers to the profits that you would receive; the second refers to the profits that the other station would receive. Thus, when you both keep your prices constant, you both earn $1,200 that week. A station that cuts when the other stays constant will earn $1,600; the station remaining constant will earn $400. If both stations cut their prices, they both will earn only $800. Eventually, you and your competitors will come to your senses, prices will increase to their old, identical levels, and the Gas Station Game will start over again.

The Gas Station Game is not only like the Game of Major League Sports, it's also like the Airline Game, where (1) one airline will cut fares to increase volume, (2) other airlines will follow suit, and (3) eventually the old, higher prices will return.

What if you were actually playing the Gas Station Game? What would you do? Would you ever cut your prices first?

Let's suppose that your main concern is profits—an easy assumption. You're in business to make money and more is better than less. That sounds simple enough. But what it also means is that you should not be concerned about how the other station does. Whether they do well or badly should be of no concern to you, unless it affects your profits.

In particular, you don't have to do better than they do. You can do very well even if they do well, too. The difficulty here is that we tend to be very competitive: We want to beat the other person, in this case, the other gas station. If we get $1,600 one week, not only will we be happy about the increase in our profits, but we might also take pleasure in the fact that, at least for a week, we beat the other station to the punch—and they made much less than we did. Unfortunately, if we let this competitive motive affect our decisions, we sometimes do worse than if we focused strictly on doing well for ourselves. Hurting the other person sometimes means sacrificing some of our own gains. But we often don't see this until it's too late. Let's see how it plays out.

DYNAMIC INTERPLAY

When groups of people play the Gas Station Game, they almost always have trouble deciding on their first choice. If you were playing this game, you would always want to ask yourself, How tempted is the other station by the possibility of a $1,600 payoff? In the original prisoner's dilemma, that question concerns the temptation to avoid jail altogether and go free. It can be very tempting. If the other station's owners are not tempted, it's safe to keep your own price constant. But if they are, it would be much better to cut your own price before they cut theirs; you don't want to get stuck with the higher price for a week.

This difficult choice becomes even more difficult when you realize that you can't communicate with the other station—it's against the law to fix prices. So you can't really know for sure that you can trust them to keep their price constant. They can't promise that they will, and neither can you.

What would happen if you cut your price? The other station would almost certainly follow by cutting theirs, even if they had kept their price constant the first time. By cutting your price, you will almost certainly be contributing to bad feelings. At the same time, if you don't cut your price and they cut theirs, you're in *worse* shape; not only will there be bad feelings, but you've also taken a loss.

The question, then, still stands: Do you trust them to act as you hope they will? Or do you protect yourself and cut your price?

A small voice in the back of your head may tell you that you should trust and believe in each other, even if you can't communicate. Another small voice, however, may simultaneously tell you that you shouldn't trust anyone. If you don't know them or what they're like, you might be inclined to be self-protective. If you cut your price, however, and the other station keeps theirs constant, they will think that you were being greedy. They may think that you cut your price to *hurt* them. And if that happens, how will you be able to ask them to forgive you and to forget what happened?

Because the first choice is such a dilemma, there is no truly typical response. When people think they will only be playing the game one time, they cut their price more often than they keep it constant. Knowing that you will be playing more than once, however, increases the likelihood of the cooperative, keep-your-price-constant choice. When groups play the Gas Station Game, they know they will make a series of choices. They also get the unexpected opportunity to communicate with one another directly after a couple of rounds of choices (even though this is technically illegal). They don't know how long the game will last, however, until just before the end.

A continuing relationship engenders much more cooperation than one that is going to end. Since the past affects both the present and the future, both you and the owners of the other gas station know that your current choices will affect each other's future choices.

If your profits are good and you know that the game will continue for some time, long-term cooperation is possible, even without communication. Indeed, a cooperative equilibrium can develop; both sides may find themselves in a stable situation with no need to change. That can only happen, however, when you both expect the game to continue.

STRATEGIES

When people play the Gas Station Game and both groups keep their prices constant on their first choices, they usually keep them constant for some time. They realize that there is no long-run benefit in cutting; they have something like a good working relationship, even without communicating; and their temptations to defect for the $1,600 payoff are reduced, at least for the moment. They have fallen into a cooperative equilibrium.

The temptations to defect, however, do not disappear. Some groups resist and go through the entire exercise, knowing when it's going to end, and still choose to keep their prices constant. We call these unusual groups consistent cooperators.

Many of the groups that start out cooperatively feel that the temptation to cut their price increases over trials. They figure that the game is going to end sometime and they don't want to be the ones who are double-crossed. *Or* they are simply tempted by the payoffs and want to reap as much as possible by double-crossing the other group, as close to the end of the game as possible. There's no way to tell these two kinds of groups apart, because the double-crossers try to say that they were just defending themselves. Other groups still perceive them as double-crossers, regardless of what they say.

Pairs that begin with one group choosing to cut and the other choosing to keep constant usually have a very hard time getting to mutually cooperative $1,200 payoffs. Each side justifies its actions with predictable arguments. The group that cut absolves itself from guilt by saying, "We couldn't talk to you, so we didn't know what you would do." When they are able to talk to each other later in the game, they are usually reluctant to take less profit, down to $400, to let the other group get $1,600 and get back to even. "Those choices are water over the dam. We can't change them now," they say.

Groups that keep their prices constant and get burned often want the other group to make amends before they commit to further cooperative choices: "Prove that you are willing to be cooperative by letting us cut our price while you keep yours constant." Occasionally one of those groups will not be so careful; they will agree to continue cooperating when the other group promises that they will now cooperate. Many original cutters break their promise and cut their price again, adding insult to the cooperative group's previous injury. Groups who continue in this competitive behavior are usually quite proud of themselves—until they realize that they have ruined their reputations, and their long-run profits fall far short of what's otherwise possible.

Pairs who both cut their prices find it very difficult to break out of mutual noncooperation, and it gets even harder when they can communicate with each other. They both verbalize their anger and their distrust of each other and the memory of these words makes reconciliation even harder. On top of that, to improve from repeated $800 outcomes to $1,200s, one firm must usually sacrifice and take at least one $400 outcome before they can both move to constant prices. That is very risky because the other side could continue to cut its price. When neither side trusts the other, neither changes: They cut and cut and cut, on every successive choice. Neither can say anything to convince the other that they will change their actions and choose cooperatively. So even when a group wants to switch to cooperation, they soon realize that their messages have had no effect and they are left with almost no incentive to cooperate. They get stuck in a noncooperative equilibrium.

COMMUNICATING AND INTENTIONS

Most people think that communication can help alleviate conflict. This straightforward conclusion has two problems: First, as we've mentioned, angry words are remembered. Second, words that aren't binding are often disregarded.

Some groups choose to cut their prices in the early rounds of the Gas Station Game. When communication channels become available, they may talk things over and decide that they will both shift to constant prices. When they make their choices, however, at least one if not both may continue to cut their prices.

Trust is not easily established, especially when the other side has already engaged in activity that you can interpret as untrustworthy. The amazing part of this is that groups make these untrustworthy interpretations of each other even as they are interpreting their own noncooperative behavior as logical and acceptable. The opportunity to communicate verbally rarely makes this double standard disappear.

Previous research on another game, the Acme-Bolt Trucking Game, documented the dynamics of trust and communication quite clearly. In this game two players represented either the Acme or the Bolt trucking company (both fictitious). They both had to travel along the same one-lane road to make their deliveries. The problem was that they traveled the road in opposite directions. Time was important and both wanted to move along as quickly as possible. With one truck filling the road, however, another truck could not get through. If Acme (or Bolt) could pass this stretch without stopping, they earned a profit on that run. If either had to wait for the other to pass, however, they would lose so much time that they couldn't make a profit for that run. The only reasonable solution to the game was to take turns using the one-lane road: On the first play one firm would profit; on the next play the other firm would profit. The profits in a two-trial alternating sequence were not huge, but they were profits. The alternative—not coordinating smoothly—meant a certain loss.

Either Acme or Bolt (or both) also had a threat: They could occasionally lock a gate on the one-lane road and not let the other company's truck through. If one closed its gate, the other could block the road with its truck or its own gate.

When one side closed its gate, the other almost invariably retaliated. Adding the opportunity for one side to block the other led to a significant *decrease* in joint profits; giving both sides that opportunity led to even lower profits.

Most people might guess that if the two trucking firms could speak to each other, they could solve their problems and both be profitable. That idea is the basis for antitrust legislation; to protect consumers, the Justice Department doesn't let competitors collude. The results of this research, however, showed no increase in profits when communication was allowed. Instead, communication led to some groups aggravating each other even more. The trucking company representatives often got into verbal battles that made it emotionally impossible for either of them to let the other use the one-lane road. As a result, they pushed each other into bankruptcy even faster than they might have without communication. The moral is not obvious: Communication doesn't always help, especially when two bargainers have gotten off on the wrong foot.

THE DEADLINE

As we noted earlier, even cooperative groups are tempted to defect. A deadline makes this temptation more severe, as both sides know that their interaction is going to end and there will be no chance for retribution. (Groups that are choosing noncooperatively are relatively unaffected by deadlines since they have no incentive to change their choice.) Double-crossers no longer need fear revenge.

If both sides realize this, they might want to beat the other side to the punch, and be the first to cut their price. Overall profits are much better if you're the first station to cut prices rather than the second. It also means you won't feel like a sucker.

This endgame strategizing, however, contains a logical problem. As soon as you know for sure that the game is going to end, and you know that the other station knows the end point, too, temptation arises. How long will they hold out before they cut? How long should you hold out? One round? Two? Ten? The only way to be *completely sure* that you will not get burned is to cut right away, as soon as you're sure the game will ultimately end. That will mean that, after getting $1,600 once, the other group will start cutting, too. The earlier that happens, however, the more you both will lose, as more $800 payoffs will replace your previous $1,200 outcomes.

As it happens, when groups know that they are going to play the game exactly 20 trials, the first defections begin, on average, at trial number 17. At trials 18 and 19, there are lots of groups cutting their prices, and almost everyone cuts on the last trial. Not everyone does, however. Groups that have established a special relationship with each other sometimes continue to keep their price constant even on the last trial.

POSTMORTEMS

After people have played the Gas Station Game, groups that cut their prices early typically explain that once they had gained an advantage, they wanted to stay ahead. They do stay ahead of the group they are bargaining with (which has no recourse but to choose noncooperatively—anything else would be suicidal). But they earn very poor profits, especially compared with more cooperative groups. This is a perfect example of the problem with competitive behavior. By continually trying to stay ahead, they lose a golden opportunity to do better. The groups who follow this strategy *invariably* do worse than cooperative groups.

The simple strategy of two stations keeping their prices constant is far superior to almost all other strategies. Sometimes a group will do better, but only if they can guess the exact timing of their last choice and double-cross the other group right at the end. The fact that this sometimes happens, completely due to luck, is very unfortunate; it reinforces the underlying temptations and heightens the dilemma in the Gas Station Game. It's best to choose cooperatively, *if* the other side will, too. The difficulty, and the dilemma, is that you can't do it alone; *both* sides must repeatedly resist temptation and risk the possibility that the other group will defect.

The Gas Station Game is one of many variations of the prisoner's dilemma game. Cutting your price is just like confessing; keeping your price constant is like keeping your mouth shut. The Gas Station and the prisoner's dilemma games are examples of *mixed-motive* games: Both parties can do well if they work together by cooperating, or they can try to gain an advantage over each other by competing. The fact that elements of both cooperation and competition are simultaneously present makes for the mixed motives and the inherent complexity in these (and most other) games.

The Gas Station and prisoner's dilemma games are also examples of the Individual-Group Game. As social animals, we always get involved in groups. Whenever that happens, as it frequently does, we can choose to work for the group (advancing the joint outcome) or to work for ourselves. When everyone in a group contributes (i.e., acts cooperatively), everyone benefits. If some people act individualistically, however, they keep what they might have contributed to the group and they also share in what everyone else has contributed. It's the classic distinction between "givers" and "takers." It's the basis for the conclusion that "nice guys finish last."

When we play the Individual-Group Game, we must make a difficult decision to stick our necks out and do more than the minimum necessary, hoping everyone else will also, or to pull back, to either protect ourselves from others' individualism or to gain from their foolish contributions.

People who don't cooperate are often called "free riders":

Their benefits depend on other people making cooperative contributions. In the variation of the Individual-Group Game called the Dilemma of Romance, two people who are attracted to each other choose how much they will contribute to their relationship. Both can have many reasons to hold back and not give much of themselves. As a result, the person who gives more may ultimately receive less. The choices in all these games—the Gas Station Game, the prisoner's dilemma, the Individual-Group Game, and the Dilemma of Romance—as well as in partnership games and other group interactions, are all quite similar. When we play them, we face dilemmas: We choose between two options, both having potentially negative consequences. That's the definition of a dilemma, and that's what makes them so tough.

Dilemmas that fit the requirements for a prisoner's dilemma have often been described as follows. The first word in each pair is person number 1's outcome; the second is person numbers 2's.

		Person 2	
		Cooperates	Noncooperates
Person 1	Cooperates	Reward, Reward	Sucker/Saint, Traitor
	Noncooperates	Traitor, Sucker/Saint	Punish, Punish

If both parties cooperate, they are rewarded; if they both defect, they are punished. If one cooperates when the other defects, the cooperator is the Sucker—or the Saint, depending on your point of view—and the noncooperator is a Traitor. In true prisoner's dilemma games, the Traitor payoff exceeds Rewards, which exceeds Punishments, which exceeds the Saint or Sucker payoff.

Not surprisingly, expectations play a big role in how people respond to these dilemmas. If one person defects when the other expected cooperation, the pair faces a major crossroads. If one of two business partners, for instance, doesn't contribute as much as the other thought she would, they may have to work out a whole new business arrangement. When two people both contribute substantially to a growing relationship, romance can flourish. Unfulfilled expectations, however, require negotiations. If they can't resolve the problems that follow a Sucker-Traitor outcome, it can signal the end to short-term and even long-term romances, to other kinds of partnerships, and to any continuation of mutual cooperation in prisoner's dilemma or Individual-Group games.

A REAL GAS STATION GAME

As a teenager in the 1960s, I particularly enjoyed it when gas stations got enmeshed in price wars. Compared with today's prices, gasoline was very cheap: Thirty-five cents a gallon was typical. Even with such seemingly low prices, stations often fought over prices, trying to beat nearby stations by cutting their prices more and more. Savings of as much as 10 or 15 cents a gallon were not uncommon.

With the oil crisis in the early 1970s, price wars seemed to disappear. Recently, however, I was driving on a two-lane highway in central Illinois and came across a station that was selling gasoline for 60 cents a gallon. I stopped and filled my tank and, while signing the credit card slip, asked the woman behind the counter why the price was so low. She said I should have been there two weeks ago—the price was only 42 cents then.

She seemed happy to tell me more about how it had happened. The other station (there was only one other station in town) had decided to boost its business by cutting prices. She and her family decided that they weren't going to lose business, so they cut their prices, too. Pretty soon both of them were cutting their prices, almost every day. (They didn't have to wait for franchise approval.) Before you knew it, she said, prices were down to 40 cents a gallon. Then she smiled and looked up at me and said, "We waited them out. They couldn't hold out as long as we did, so they had to start raising their price or go out of business." She was really pleased with herself. She seemed to feel that they had won the war—and maybe they had. (Although at what a cost?) As I drove out of town, I made sure to drive by the other station to see what they were charging. The sign said 61 cents a gallon.

TEA FOR TWO AND TIT FOR TAT

Robert Axelrod, a political scientist at the University of Michigan, has made some fascinating discoveries in his research on prisoner's dilemma games. His book, *The Evolution of Cooperation,* presents an encouraging outlook on how people can play these difficult, mixed-motive games.

He ran two computer tournaments where people submitted their strategies for a simple prisoner's dilemma game that would be repeated many times. Everyone's strategy was paired against everyone else's and their outcomes were tabulated. The winner in both tournaments (there were sixteen contestants in the first, sixty-eight in the second) was the eminent scholar and peace advocate, Anatol Rapoport.

Rapoport submitted the simplest strategy of all, Tit for Tat, which chooses cooperatively on the first trial and, on every subsequent trial, chooses exactly as the other player did on his previous choice. Thus, if we use C to denote a cooperative choice and N to denote a noncooperative choice, Tit for Tat would respond to choices of

$$C - C - N - N - C - N - C - C$$

with

$$C - C - C - N - N - C - N - C.$$

Tit for Tat's next choice would also be cooperative, as that was the other player's last choice.

Axelrod analyzed Tit for Tat's phenomenal success in great

detail. He concluded that it is *nice, retaliatory, forgiving,* and *clear.* It is nice because it never chooses noncooperatively first. It is retaliatory because it immediately reacts against noncooperative choices. It's forgiving because it imposes no penalties for previous noncooperation: As soon as the other person returns to cooperative play, Tit for Tat does also. It's clear because it never varies from this simple pattern.

Tit for Tat *trains* the other player to be cooperative: It punishes noncooperation and rewards cooperative choices. Perceptive opponents soon realize that a player using Tit for Tat will not be tricked into anything other than a consistent pattern of reflective choices. Tit for Tat is never nasty, never cruel; it's as dependable as a friend can be. If you find yourself playing such a game with someone who is playing Tit for Tat, you might as well cooperate; it will be very profitable, for both of you. It's not moralistic; it's not demanding; it's beautifully simple.

Tit for Tat is like the old strategy, If you scratch my back, I'll scratch yours. But it's also more than that; on the negative side, it's also, An eye for an eye, a tooth for a tooth. People are quite good at scratching each other's backs in cooperative relationships; they're also quite good at extracting revenge immediately in competitive relationships. The beauty of Tit for Tat is that it combines both strategies, without any emotional baggage. It doesn't get personal.

A paradox about Tit for Tat is that it never does better than its opponent. Because it starts cooperatively and then responds to what the other player does, it can never do better than they do. It does as well if they both cooperate continually, but it can never do better. When it won the tournament, Tit for Tat trained its opponents to cooperate so well that, on average, it did better than any of the other strategies. Here is a real lesson for people who are inclined to be competitive, who want to defeat their opponent: You don't ever have to beat any individual opponent to still do very well, and maybe even win the entire game. (Greg LeMond won the 1990 Tour de France bicycle race in similar fashion: He didn't win any single leg of the race; instead, he did well enough in every leg to win overall.) In the normal competition of most business interactions, this strategy looks mediocre, humble, and not very effective. But it's lack of flash only hides the fact that *Tit for Tat works,* and works very well over the long haul.

Axelrod also pursued the possibility that the Tit for Tat strategy might be able to survive in an evolutionary sense. If we think of prisoner's dilemma games as a model for the Game of Life (or the Game of Business), could a cooperative player using the Tit for Tat strategy survive in a hostile world? Could a cooperatively oriented business survive in a competitive market infested with sharks?

Cooperation *can* survive *if* enough other cooperative players are nearby. Thus, cooperative, Tit for Tat players might move into hostile, noncooperative territory. By interacting with everyone there, they might be able to find someone else willing to cooperate and, if so, by working together, they have a chance to flourish (by doing better than the noncooperators who surround them). Without other cooperators, however, the Tit for Tat strategy will continually choose noncooperatively after being burned on its first choice. In a completely hostile place, it would begin with a poor outcome and never have a chance to regain its losses. Thus, a business that wants to diversify into new areas needs to know whether it will have any friends there to help smooth their entry. Without them, the prospects may be bleak.

Cooperators can also do well by bringing other cooperators along. They can then survive among themselves, even when they are surrounded by noncooperators. By doing so, they establish a mutually cooperative enclave that can sustain itself. In the interconnected, interdependent world of business, though, this would only work if the invading enclave was self-sufficient right from the start.

Finding other cooperators in hostile territory reduces the number of compatriots you need to bring along. Combining the two strategies—entering hostile markets only when you know some cooperators there, and bringing cooperators with you—can overcome bleakly noncooperative environments. And once cooperators get a toehold, they have an evolutionary advantage, since mutual cooperation beats mutual noncooperation.

The moral of this story is fairly simple: *If* cooperation is beneficial and others are amenable, cooperative choices can be very rewarding. Two parties who start out noncooperatively will have a hard time getting back to cooperative choices. At the same time, however, cooperative choices may be able to change the nature of a game. (We'll see how this can work in upcoming chapters.) If the game lasts long enough, cooperators can thrive and do more than simply survive. It's so pleasant when it works that, most of the time, it's important to look for chances to cooperate.

CHAPTER 5

INFORMATION

It's no fun to be seduced by an economist. There are more great women than great men. And the worst conversation you could have is one with an expert in speech communication. Jim March, a well-known scholar in the social sciences, once began a presentation by saying that he would be covering these three topics. He then proceeded to argue, quite persuasively, that unpredictability is a necessary element in decision making; without it, decisions could not capture the inherent richness of the problems they are trying to solve. His talk lasted over an hour, and most of us were anxious to hear more about sexy economists, great women, and bad conversations (three topics that seemed unrelated to each other and, possibly, to the rest of his talk).

Finally he explained. The reason that it's no fun to be seduced by an economist, he said, is that economists always calculate the costs and benefits of their actions before they do anything. If they should try to seduce you, you can bet that they've already calculated that their benefits exceed their costs. As a result, their seduction attempt has no spontaneity and unpredictability and, rather than being great fun, it's no fun at all.

With regard to great women and great men, he said that, for men, socialization prescribes particular roles: Being masculine means being more forceful, less emotional, and less interpersonally perceptive. When women are socialized, on the other hand, they are not so constrained; they can be tomboys, for instance, for a long time. Their roles, although quite clear, are somewhat looser than men's. As a result, they can interpret situations in many different ways; they also have more action choices when it's time to react. Thus, they have much more of a chance to be a great person than a man.

Finally, he argued, the best part of a conversation is not only *not* knowing what the other person might say, but also *not* knowing what you yourself might say. Conversations are opportunities to discover what other people think. But they're much more important as opportunities to discover what you yourself think. Most of us don't go home in the evening, for example, and ponder the serious issues of the day by ourselves. Instead, we engage in conversations where we hear what we have to say, sometimes surprising ourselves in the process.

People who are experts in speech communication, on the other hand, really know what they're doing in conversations. This is their bread and butter. Not only are they completely sure of what they are saying before they say it, but they are also completely sure of what *we* are saying when we say it. This robs conversations of all of their spice and flair, making for truly boring interactions. In all three cases, it's unpredictability that makes things interesting.

When we begin a negotiation, we typically face some unpredictability: We may not know exactly what the other person wants, even if we know what we want ourselves. They may not know what we really want, either, especially if we don't know what we want.

If we want to buy some object, say a piece of property, we probably won't know the lowest final price that the seller will actually accept. If unpredictability makes for spice and enjoyable interactions, then negotiations that include this kind of uncertainty—and most do—should be fun.

When a negotiation is important, however, uncertainty generates tension—whether we are bargaining for a piece of art, a house, or a used car; whether we are negotiating a merger, a takeover, or some other acquisition; or whether we simply want to persuade someone to go along with what we want to do. If the stakes are high, everyone's adrenaline flows, and unpredictability is something almost everyone tries to resolve.

If you are selling a house, you will carefully guard information that will tell a potential buyer anything about the lowest price you would accept for it. By keeping this figure ambiguous for buyers—but knowing it yourself—you would hope to get more than that minimum value.

Similarly, when two people have decided to divorce, they may try to hide financial information from their spouse. That is why we hire lawyers or divorce mediators to represent us in these disputes: They know what kinds of financial information may be hidden (for example, contributions to one person's pension or profit sharing plan by their employer) and have methods for discovering it.

Organizations whose sole purpose is to spy on others attest to the importance of resolving unpredictability. *Information is power.* That is a truism in many situations even if it's not universally true. Occasionally having more information can hurt your bargaining outcomes. But even if information is not always power, people typically act as if it were—because most of the time information *does* convey power by giving people the chance to use more effective strategies. The Information Game, which we will describe below, helps identify exactly when information is valuable and when it isn't. (Most of the time it is.)

INFORMATION AND A USED CAR

I was involved in a negotiation for a used car a few years ago. I describe it here not to show how well I negotiated, although I did do some things right. Instead, I'd like to emphasize how many different aspects of information are important in bargaining.

It was nearing the end of the year. I had just returned from spending a sabbatical in France. I had sold my old car before I left the States and planned to buy a car when I returned. I arrived a few days before Christmas to visit my parents for the holidays. I checked the local suburban newspaper and found a few cars that sounded interesting. But I wasn't really in the mood for buying a car yet.

After Christmas, I checked the paper again to see if any of the cars I was interested in were still for sale. A convertible I had seen the previous week was gone. I was disappointed, but I consoled myself by thinking that it was too expensive and too frivolous for someone who lives with Midwest winters. Three other possibilities, though, were still listed, so I called the owners and arranged to see them. My thirteen-year-old son came along to act, in his words, as my adviser.

All three cars seemed fine. The first was clearly the nicest of the three: It had air conditioning, a sunroof, AM-FM cassette stereo—the works. It also had a little feature that, for some reason, I found particularly interesting. The windshield wipers' control mechanism could be adjusted so that they would work anywhere from once every four seconds to once every twelve seconds. Why was I so intrigued? I have no idea, really. Maybe I thought that if the manufacturers paid so much attention to this little aspect of the car's design, they must have attended to the rest equally well.

With my son's urging—he liked this car, too—I went to the local library to check out how much it should be worth. The owners were asking $5,100; they said they were selling the car because they would soon be having a baby and needed something bigger. The book on used cars said that $5,100 was the average retail price. Average trade-in was $4,500; average wholesale was somewhere in between.

I called the owner back and said, first off, that I liked the car and was interested in talking more about buying it. I explained, though, that the only way I would buy it was if I was happy about everything, including the price, and that I had gone to the library to see what a fair price would be.

I revealed all of the information I had gotten at the library. I described the adjustments for air conditioning, the stereo, the sunroof, and mileage. After running through all these numbers, I said that, although they had a nice car, I thought they were asking too much and that I wouldn't be happy if I paid what they were asking. She responded by saying, "So does this mean you're going to make an offer?"

I was totally surprised by her question. I hadn't planned to make an offer. I hadn't thought that far ahead, which was not very smart on my part but may actually have been lucky. As a result, I hesitated and said, "Yes, I'll offer you forty-five hundred dollars." She said that a dealer had offered them that much, but he also said they could probably do better by selling it to a private buyer. This is where my lack of preplanning may have come in handy. I said, "Okay, I'll offer forty-five fifty." Had I made plans ahead of time, I might have raised my offer more. She said she would have to talk to her husband about it and that she would call back.

She called that evening and said that, considering the cost of their ads and other expenses, they would need $4,600 to sell the car. I said that would be fine. We made the deal, contingent on the car being inspected and approved by a mechanic.

I went to their place the next day and, on my way, saw a repair shop near their home. As I didn't know any mechanics in the area, I hoped that this place was respectable and would do a good job of checking the car for me. They advertised that they specialized in European and Japanese cars; I thought that was a good sign. But I really knew nothing about the place or its reputation.

As I was picking up the car, she mentioned that she thought the brakes needed some work, so I shouldn't be surprised if the mechanic mentioned that.

The repair shop started their buyer's check for me right away. The man in charge had a German accent, which wasn't unusual in this neighborhood. The problem, however, was that we didn't communicate well. Every so often he would report a fairly minor problem with the car, one being that the brakes needed some work. Each time he reported something, I nodded and said, "Okay."

I thought I was just telling him that I understood; he thought I was telling him to do the work. As a result, he and his mechanics made all the repairs he had mentioned. Unfortunately, in the meantime, I contacted the owner only to see if she would agree to split the cost of the brake work. I never mentioned the other seemingly minor problems with the car since I didn't realize they were all being fixed. As it turned out, the buyer's check took a long time—which makes sense, since they were tuning up the car and adjusting the valves *and* fixing the brakes!

As you might guess, I am not an expert in automobile mechanics. Although my negotiation for the purchase of the car went well, my interaction with the car repair people—another negotiation—did not go so well. The bill for their work was almost $200; the owner was only obliged to pay $35. Although I probably needed all this work done on the car eventually, I might not have needed it right away and I might have been able to get the work done for less. My lack of knowledge about automobile mechanics—and my lack of ability in translating German-accented English—shows how important information can be.

Other information about the car, however, was very valuable. First, I knew that the car had been advertised for at least two weeks and that it was Christmas season, when many people are short of money. I thought I could get it for a good price.

Second, the information from the library was also very handy. Without it, who knows where I would have started the negotiations. I might have alienated the sellers if I started too low, or paid too much if I started too high. Either way, I could have screwed things up so much that I wouldn't have purchased a fine car and the owners would have missed a sale.

Ignorance may be bliss but having information is even better. Then you can determine whether you really should be happy with an agreement. "What you don't know can't hurt you" is the basis for blissful ignorance. In negotiation, what you don't know *can* hurt you, sometimes quite a lot. You can end up making a very bad bargain for yourself. It almost always pays to get as much information as you can *before* you negotiate.

What's strange is that people have a tendency to gather information about a negotiation *after* rather than before they bargain. At the same time, they often distort what they find. Rather than being skeptical, for instance, people begin to believe advertisements that say that their new car is terrific, even when there is little factual basis for the claim.

On the other hand, sometimes people find out later that they've made a bad bargain—that they bought the wrong car for an inflated price. Then it becomes very clear that what you don't know can hurt you.

There's a downside to information, even when it helps you reach better agreements. The more you know, the more it might take for you to really be happy. As a teenager, I worked as a caddy at a golf course. The people I caddied for were financially well-off, unlike me. But by working for them, I learned about high-quality golf equipment. As a result, I wouldn't be happy playing with anything else. My friends and I were nowhere close to being wealthy, but you could never tell that from our golf clubs. We always had top-of-the-line equipment because we always had top-of-the-line information.

Thus, information and happiness interact; information lets you know whether you should be happy. That applies to business deals, to romances, and to negotiations of all kinds. It also applies to the Information Game, which I will finally describe below. At the same time, more information allows people to be better negotiators (and, in most instances, better golfers, better managers, and better lovers). Although increased information might lead to some sacrifice in happiness, the gains usually outweigh the losses. As a general rule, more information is much better than less.

THE INFORMATION GAME

The Information Game is based strictly on how much information two bargainers have about each other's potential profits. If you were to play the Information Game, you would be assigned a high or a low prize. If you had the high prize ($500), your opponent would always have the low prize ($20). Likewise, if you were the $20 player, your opponent would always be bargaining for a $500 prize.

You win your prize if you bargain well *and* you're lucky in the lottery that's conducted after your negotiations. You and your opponent will not be bargaining over your prizes but, instead, over one hundred lottery tickets. To reach agreement, you must decide how to divide the hundred tickets. The tickets determine your chances of winning your prize, so everyone tries to get as many lottery tickets as he can. Let's assume that you are the $20 player and you reached an agreement giving you sixty lottery tickets. That means that you would have a sixty percent chance of winning your prize. You would spin a "wheel of fortune" with numbers from 1 to 100 on it. If any number from 1 to 60 comes up, you win your prize. If any number over 60 results, you may have bargained well but bad luck would leave you with no prize. Your opponent would also spin the wheel, and would win her prize ($500) if any number from 1 to 40 came up, since she finished your negotiation with 40 tickets. More tickets always mean a better chance of winning your prize. But that is also true for the person you would be bargaining with, so it's not so easy to get a lot of tickets. And if you disagree, neither of you will have any chance of winning your prizes.

You always know the value of your prize. Depending on the situation, you may also know the value of the other bargainer's prize, too. Four different information situations are possible:

1. Neither of you knows the other's prize.
2. You know that the other bargainer's prize is $500 but she doesn't know yours is $20.
3. She knows that your prize is $20 but you don't know hers.
4. You both know each other's prizes.

You always know the value of your prize; you may know the value of hers. But you don't know whether she knows your prize. And she doesn't know whether you know hers. You can tell each other your prize values if you wish, or you can keep that information to yourself. But even if you reveal your prizes, neither of you can reveal it with certainty. You can't really determine whether the information you get is accurate; your opponent can't either. It's like a car dealer who shows you the invoice on the car you are going to buy. Whether it's the *actual* invoice is not always clear.

Factual information about the other bargainer's prize, then, can be very valuable. If your prize was $20 and you knew that the other person's prize was $500, you could demand much more than a 50-50 split, since your prize was so low. If, on the other hand, your prize was $500 and you knew that the other person's was $20, you might keep quiet about your prize to improve your chances of getting it.

You always want to get as many lottery tickets as you can, regardless of your prize. So while you may try to get information about the other bargainer's prize, you will always be trying for more lottery tickets, because after your negotiations are over, you win your prize only if you win your lottery, and more tickets give you a better chance.

WHAT HAPPENS

The no-information condition, where neither bargainer knows the other's prize, is the normal state of affairs in most negotiations. We often know quite a lot about our own values and benefits, but we rarely know very much about other bargainers' possible outcomes. And usually they keep us in the dark, too.

Let's assume that you have the $20 prize and you don't know the other person's prize. You can assume anything you want; you can wonder what her prize might be, but you really don't know. You may be able to discover something about it during negotiations, but even if she tells you the value of her prize, you can't be sure that what she tells you is true. All you really know is that, if you win your lottery, you will win $20.

When the negotiations begin, you ask for ninety-five of the lottery tickets. Your opponent can react in two ways, by being offended with your request or by laughing at your chutzpah.

Let's say that she says she would love to have ninety-five tickets as well, but that she would be more than happy with eighty-five. Now that you've begun, you can see that this negotiation is not going to be easy: Your interests and hers are diametrically opposed.

During discussion, you ask her what her prize is. She responds by asking, "What's yours?" You try to argue that you were the first to ask, so she should be the first to answer. She responds by saying that if you tell her your prize, she'll tell you hers. (This sounds a lot like a game you used to play as a kid.) You finally relent and tell her your prize is $20. She says that hers is about the same. Does this information help? (Since we know that her prize was actually $500, we know it shouldn't help. But if you were involved in this negotiation and didn't know her prize, you might be affected by it.)

With the time deadline rapidly approaching, you concede and ask for only sixty-five tickets. She concedes to sixty. You both go back and forth, making small concessions. You think that you will end up at 50-50, but you're not sure and you don't want her to have any advantage that she shouldn't have. Neither of you has a convincing argument that would lead the other to give you more than 50-50, so you seem doomed to settle for half. You take things to the last second, and then you both concede and accept 50-50.

Though the pattern of these negotiations might change, the outcome is almost always the same: When you don't have any information about the other person's prize and they don't have any information about yours, people generally settle for 50-50 even if they take the negotiations right up to the last second (which happens frequently).

What if you were in a similar situation, but now she knows the value of your prize but you still don't know hers? You realize that this may put you at a disadvantage, so you toughen your resolve.

The bargaining pattern in this situation often begins just like the no-information situation. At some point, however, her information may come into play, even though she doesn't mention it. The only difference you notice during bargaining is that now your opponent is slightly less intransigent. When you continue to push your position, she bends more than you expected. In fact, she offers a 50-50 split before you do. Although you find this puzzling, time is again beginning to run out, and you argue that you will only settle for 60-40. Strangely enough, she is not angry about this, but still pushes for 50-50. As time runs down, you say that you would accept 58-42. She offers you 52-48 expressing a willingness to settle for less than fifty herself. At the last moment, you both settle on 54-46, your advantage.

You finish the negotiations with pride. The fact that you did better than 50-50 is only a reflection of what a good bargainer you must be. (At least that's what you tell yourself.) What you don't realize is that your better-than-50-50 outcome is a direct result of her having more information and knowing that her prize is substantially larger than yours.

Giving you a slightly better deal than 50-50 is not horrendous to her; it still assures her of a good chance at $500, which looks pretty good compared to your slightly higher chance at only $20. When the person in the first negotiation didn't know your prize (and may have doubted you when you told her it was $20), she found it much easier to take a strong stand, even though her prize was also $500. No information was actually a luxury: She did better and had no reason to feel bad about it. Having information in this second negotiation, however, made it harder for her to deny that she was getting the better end of the deal. Whether we label these feelings guilt, or rooting for the underdog, or seeking fair play, knowing that your own prize is bigger may, and often does, hurt a negotiator's ability to bargain toughly.

The moral of this story is clear. Yes, information is power; it is almost always valuable; but if it tells a negotiator that he already has a good deal, it makes it harder for him to bargain as hard as he might have if he didn't know what a good deal he had.

Information that tells you that you have a bad deal, on the other hand, makes you bargain harder. Whether your harder bargaining is effective depends on how you use this information. Let's see how that works.

TURNING THE INFORMATION TABLES

Let's say that your prize is still $20, but now you know that the other person's prize is $500. She doesn't know that you have this information and she has no information about you.

At the very beginning, you let her know that you know her prize. You want things to be open and clear: She has a better deal than you do; you want her to know that you know it. You also say that since your prize is worse than hers, you should get more lottery tickets. You explain that since your prize is $20 and hers is $500, to make things more equitable you should get at least a 96-percent chance in the lottery and she should get at most 4 percent. By doing this, your expected value and hers would be the same: Your 96-percent chance of getting $20 converts to an expected value of $19.20 (.96 times $20); her expected value is about the same, but even a little higher, at $20 (.04 times $500). Thus, you argue, this is more than fair.

You are quite pleased with your logic and your argument. You have used your information effectively. You fully expect her to be unhappy with your argument, but she should have a hard time fighting with it.

For some reason, though, she doesn't see it that way. Instead, she says that 50-50 is the only fair agreement. She says that neither of you had anything to do with the prize distribution, so the prizes are irrelevant. A 50-50 agreement is fair and she won't accept anything less. In addition, she says, who knows whether your prize is really $20?

This is not what you expected—in fact, it's much worse than you expected. Not only has she disagreed with your logical argument, but she's raised the possibility that you are lying about the value of your prize. That makes you mad. So you tell her that you are telling the truth, that you are not a liar, and that 96-4 is the only outcome that's really fair: Coming close to equal expected values gives you an almost equal chance at doing well in this game. Anything else just isn't fair.

She responds by saying that even if you are telling the truth, the only fair agreement is 50-50. That makes you even madder.

"*Even* if I am telling the truth," you say to yourself. By this time, the deadline is approaching. So far neither of you has conceded anything at all. Also, even if you didn't believe your own arguments wholeheartedly in the beginning, you believe them now. You like the way they sounded; this is how you really feel. So you simply state that you aren't budging from 96-4; she responds by saying that she's not moving from 50-50. As time expires, one or the other of you may collapse and concede to the other; but often neither of you does, so you end up with a disagreement, leaving both of you with no chance to win your prizes.

Here we have a situation where you thought you put your information advantage to good use: You presented a logical, coherent argument in terms that should not have generated any unexpected hostility. Nevertheless, the situation blew up in your face and you weren't able to agree.

Experience shows that this situation—where the disadvantaged bargainer has information about the advantaged bargainer—leads to many disagreements. Informed, disadvantaged players tend to take a strong stand. Both sides take societally accepted positions, arguing for equality (50-50) or for equal expected values, and making a concession may feel like you've violated your principles.

In addition, having one bargainer tell the truth and not be believed by the other doesn't help. Like the Game of Chicken, which we will discuss later, disagreement is the worst possible outcome in this game. When pride is pricked, however, such irrational disagreements become more likely. Again, we see that emotions can be very powerful and can interfere with a strictly rational negotiation process.

STRATEGIES

Earlier we discussed the situation where the $500 players knew both prizes but kept their information quiet. Other $500 players in this situation misrepresented their prize, trying to use their information to even greater advantage. They would acknowledge that they knew the other players' prize was $20. At the same time, they "revealed" the value of their prize, typically saying that it was also $20.

Before we go further, let's stop and analyze this revelation strategically. (We'll discuss the fact that this strategy is unethical in a later chapter.) If you were going to lie about your prize, why would you say that it's $20? Why not go further and say that it's only $5 or even less? When bargainers say that their prize is the same as the other bargainer's, they give themselves no real advantage. Instead, it's a *disadvantage,* since the other bargainer might detect the lie. Thus, people who presented incorrect information were hurt by how they implemented that strategy. To do better, they needed to present their situation as much worse.

Even beyond the ethics of this situation, the moral is quite clear: Misinformation is hazardous material, and ambitious but inexpert bargainers are very likely to get burned when they use this strategy.

Toy Drums

Several years ago, my brother and I engaged in a series of information-relevant negotiations in Paris. While wandering around the city, we ran into a man selling little toy drums. They had natural-looking skins and were attached to a wooden handle. Two strings with little balls on the ends were attached to the top. When you twisted the handle, the balls would swing around and hit the drum, making a nice sound. Spinning the handle back and forth would beat the drum repeatedly. We were both taken by their novelty and sound.

When Tom asked how much they cost, the man said 25 francs. Tom shook his head and said, "Seven." His voice was firm and serious. The salesman, also shaking his head and sounding serious, said, "Twenty-five." Tom stuck at seven. Finally, the seller came down, and came down, and came down. Tom gave in at 10 francs. I thought he had done quite well and

I bought one, too. Only afterward did I realize that they would make good gifts for my children. So I was on the lookout for another one.

A couple of nights later we went to Montmartre. We began at the quiet end of the boulevard and walked toward the Place Pigalle. Along the way we ran into several drum salesmen. They were asking 25 francs for their drums. We wanted to be on our way and didn't want to stop, so we kept going, without doing any negotiating or buying.

The farther we walked, the more lively the street became. More lights, more shops, more people—and more men selling these little drums. At the same time, the price escalated. By the time we were at Pigalle, the asking price was 50 francs!

We returned to our hotel without bargaining for another drum. The next day we went to the flea market, reputed to be the biggest in the world. When we stopped for lunch, another drum salesman walked by. I stopped him and asked about the price of a drum. I don't remember what price he started at. I do remember, though, that I had decided to pay exactly 10 francs for it. I thought that was a reasonable price; we had paid it before, it probably represented a profit for the seller, and it was only a little over a dollar. All in all, it seemed like a fair exchange.

I offered him 10 francs. He groaned and repeated his asking price. I was seated comfortably in this outdoor café and I simply repeated my offer of 10 francs—over and over again. After a little while, the people at the other tables were paying attention and getting quite entertained by my casual negotiating style, especially as the seller was working hard to get me to raise my price. I simply smiled and said, "Ten francs," repeatedly. Finally, he gave in. He turned his face away as he handed over the drum and took my money. I'm pretty sure he was disgusted that he hadn't done better, especially with a crowd watching.

In retrospect, I should have started lower. By not making any concessions I probably made the seller lose face. Had I started at 5 francs and slowly worked my way up to 10, he may have enjoyed the interaction much more. That way we both would have conceded. As things happened, however, the seller made all the concessions.

When I related my story to the negotiations class I taught in Paris a few years later, they told me that I should have only paid 5 francs. I was already sure that I could have paid less than 10 francs, but what would I have saved? And what additional pain would I have inflicted on the seller, who really did have to work hard just to sell it for 10?

I was quite happy with the deal I had struck. I was well informed before going in, much like the $500 player in the Information Game who knew both prizes. I didn't have enough information or enough of an advantage to misrepresent my own payoff, though, even if I had wanted to. But I did feel that I was in a tremendously advantageous position, and I used my information to strike what I considered to be a fair deal. Had the seller seen right away that I was not going to budge, he probably would have sold me the drum immediately for 10 francs. As it was, he understandably assumed that sooner or later I would concede and offer more than 10 francs. Instead, I violated a long-held, almost universal norm of reciprocating concessions.

At the time, I felt that I had simply stuck to what I thought was fair. I knew the situation. I knew myself. I knew what would make me happy with the deal. I even found out later that 10 francs was a fair price. From a strictly outcome-oriented perspective, things worked out well. Both people probably got a good deal. From a process-oriented perspective, however, I could have been kinder by starting out tougher. The monetary outcome would not have changed, but the outcome isn't everything in bargaining—neither of us should have had to feel bad or be embarrassed in what was, objectively, a mutually beneficial exchange.

Had this been a business deal, with much more money involved, I probably would never be able to deal with the same seller easily again. I had subtly expressed disrespect for him, his wares, and his negotiating. If I had to deal with him again, I would probably lose out: Negotiations might be strained; we might miss a good deal together; the intangibles might all be negative. Thus, although I may have done well in the short term by offering a fair price and sticking to it, I may have poisoned the water for the long term—and only because of interpersonal, not financial issues.

A PIG IN A POKE

Almost all of the time information is power. Knowing what's going on allows us to determine the best course of action. An absence of information keeps us in the dark about bargaining strategies that might be effective.

The phrase "a pig in a poke" is a perfect example of the importance of information, and how easily you can get burned if you don't have it. In medieval times, farmers would often come to market with a baby pig in a sack (a "poke"), slung over their shoulders. Baby pigs were quite valuable and could fetch a good price. Scoundrels soon saw this as a golden opportunity. Rather than a pig, they often put a cat (a worthless animal at the time) in their poke and sold it as a pig. Unsuspecting buyers soon learned to beware of "a pig in a poke."

My negotiations in the Old City in Jerusalem, described in the first chapter, also attest to the value of information. When I bargained for the funky little bag, I had no information about its market value and I may have paid too much for it. When I bargained for the rug, I didn't need it and could take advantage of the fact that I was less involved. I also accumulated a lot of information about the market value of similar rugs. Thus, when the second rug dealer tried to sell me another rug, I was very well prepared.

Sometimes information can hinder us in bargaining, particularly if it tells us that we are going to do much better in a negotiation than our opponent. This kind of information may limit how hard we bargain. Since we aren't totally self-centered, completely hedonistic carnivores, what happens to others is information that affects our strategic calculations. Thus, when we know we are making a killing, we may pull back and relax our bargaining strategies. By sacrificing some of our own desired outcomes, however, we may assume an unnecessary burden, one that our opponents might be able to avoid if they had to, that is, if we continued to bargain hard. Thus, by pushing for what we think is fair, we might generate an outcome that sacrifices gains for both parties.

Usually, however, more information gives us the opportunity to formulate better strategies that will promote our own outcomes, and sometimes even our opponents', too. More information is truly advantageous, not just because it provides us with the opportunity to maximize our own individual outcomes, but, rather, because it allows us to take into consideration everyone's interests in reaching a negotiated solution.

CHAPTER 6

THE
ULTIMATUM
GAME

Someone you don't know offers you $1.11, with no strings attached. Would you take it? *Spy* magazine made that offer to fifty-eight "well-known, well-heeled Americans." The magazine simply sent them a check for $1.11 and waited to see who would cash it. Twenty-six, including Cher, Michael Douglas, Shirley MacLaine, and Kurt Vonnegut, cashed the check. They all received a follow-up check for 64 cents, with the explanation that it covered "a computer error." Thirteen cashed it this time. They were then sent a check for 13 cents. Among the people who cashed all three? Donald Trump.

Clearly there were some strings attached to *Spy*'s offer; people's responses provided the magazine with another goofy story. But what if someone offered you $1.11, without any strings. What would you do? In today's world, there are rarely no strings attached. Most people have learned that there is no free lunch. But, theoretically, if someone offered you money, why wouldn't you take it?

Let's play this out a little further. Imagine that you were actually offered money by someone you didn't know and whom you would never meet. She was given an amount of money and asked to divide it with you. You don't know how much she was given, and she can't tell you. (Everything is done anonymously.)

You are told that the task was simply to divide the money with you, in any way this person liked. You would then have the opportunity to accept or reject what she offered. If you accepted, you kept what you were offered and she kept the rest. If you rejected, you would both get nothing. Would you take a dollar? If not, would you take $5? If you took the dollar, would you have taken a quarter? A dime? A penny?

Economic theory says that you should take any amount, since some money is better than nothing. (This assumes that you value money.) Psychological theory would say pretty much the same thing. You can't know whether the other person is being fair, since you don't know how much is being divided. You might reject very small amounts if they are meaningless to you. But a dollar still has some value to almost everyone.

What is the smallest amount you would accept? Before I tell you what many people do, let's change the scene.

TAKE IT OR LEAVE IT

You and Pat are walking down the street together. You had been acquaintances at school and had kept in touch occasionally. You knew each other reasonably well. It was a normal everyday afternoon until an older couple stopped you with an intriguing proposition. They offered the two of you $100,000 if you could decide how you would divide the money. You had to decide in less than three minutes. You and Pat were flabbergasted and, to say the least, a bit incredulous. You asked the older couple sarcastically, "This is something for a television show, right?" But the older couple looked at you seriously and said, "No, this is just between us and the two of you. If you can decide how you will divide the money, we will give it to you." Then they opened the bag they were carrying and showed you a bundle of nice, new $1,000 bills. Then they said, "Your time starts now."

If we were to think of this actually happening, most of us would say to ourselves, "Well, this is really nice. Both of us will walk away with fifty thousand dollars. This is some great deal." Almost everyone thinks this will be the outcome, just as almost everyone divided

$100 into two piles of $50 in the Silent Bargaining Quiz in Chapter 2. So you turned to Pat with a big smile and said, "So, Pat, what do you say? How about fifty thousand dollars each?" You fully expected Pat to accept; most people would.

But Pat had different ideas. She said, "Gee, I'm really sorry, but my mother has been very sick lately. We wanted her to get an operation to correct her condition, but it was way too expensive and her insurance wouldn't cover it. In fact, the operation costs eighty thousand dollars. This deal these people are offering us is too good to be true. It means that my mother will be able to live comfortably again, without pain or without worrying about dying. So I'll take eighty thousand dollars so she can have her operation and you can still get twenty thousand. I won't settle for anything less. She needs this operation too much."

What would you do now? Your time is ticking away rapidly. It's almost up and you have to decide. Pat wants $80,000—which means you get only $20,000. She says she doesn't care about anything less. For Pat, it's $80,000 or nothing. Does that mean that it's $20,000 or nothing for you? Will you accept that?

The general question here is, what do you do when someone gives you an ultimatum? Many negotiations often come down to one side making a final offer. Do you get angry and feel offended and wonder why the person thought you would ever succumb to such a rude proposal? Or do you take a minute and calculate what's best for you and determine what to do?

Take it or leave it is a choice we often heard when we were children. As adults, we rarely ever hear it put that way. But ultimatums still play a big part in bargaining, especially when the bargaining is competitive. At any time during a long negotiation, one side can terminate further bargaining and make an ultimatum. The Ultimatum Game, described next, models this endgame interaction. We'll get to the end of the story with Pat later.

THE ULTIMATUM GAME

If we boil down an ultimatum to its simplest form, we have the Ultimatum Game. You or another person make a take-it-or-leave-it offer dividing some amount of money. The negotiations occur very quickly: One of you divides the money; if the second person refuses the proposal, you both get nothing. If the second person accepts the proposal, you share the money, as determined by the first person. That's it.

There are several variations to this game. The first is the Unknown Amount Ultimatum Game. Here the second person doesn't know the total that is being divided; he only knows how much he is offered. Our research indicates that some people are willing to take anything, even a penny, in this game; others reject any amount less than $5. If you are in a business negotiation and you receive a take-it-or-leave-it ultimatum, and you know *nothing* about the other company's profits, any agreement that gives you a profit may seem satisfactory. In fact, people tend to adopt one of two different philosophies here: The first says to accept anything, or almost anything. The second doesn't bother with small amounts.

When people know the total that is being divided, their choices change: Knowing how much someone else will get from the deal leads to more rejections of small amounts. Thus, if someone is dividing $100 and offers the other person $5, most people reject it. Many reject $10 and even $20. People who don't know that the other person was dividing $100, on the other hand, typically accept $5, $10, or $20.

Economic theory is puzzled by these responses: Something is still better than nothing, even when you know how much is being divided. But psychological theory readily accepts people acting in this way. It may not be economically rational, but refusing free money because the division isn't fair is easily justified psychologically.

THE THINGS PEOPLE DO

When people play the basic Ultimatum Game, they flip a coin to determine who makes the proposal. The first person divides a known amount of money, say twenty dollars. The second person can accept or reject. That ends the game—it doesn't take long. It's the most basic of bargaining games.

Many people offer a 50-50 split of the money. That is a very safe strategy; almost no one rejects this deal—it's completely equal and totally fair. At the same time, the person making the offer might not be getting as much as he could.

Many people offer less than 50-50, trying to gauge just how little the other person will take without rejecting their offer and leaving them both with nothing. Clearly, as they offer less and less, the chances of the second person rejecting their offer increase.

Sooner or later, most people reject a small positive gain. In each case, they know that the other person is getting more than they are and that enters into their calculations. Economic models of rational choice imply that pride and personal values shouldn't matter: The second person should accept any positive offer. A small number of people do feel that way and will accept very small amounts. Strategically, however, they are clever enough not to reveal this to the person dividing the money.

More often, however, people will reject proposals that they feel aren't good enough. The issue here is the common question, what's fair? Some people will reject any proposal that gives them less than an equal share; they would rather walk away with nothing. One executive participating in one of my negotiation seminars argued vehemently that he would turn down a quarter of a million dollars if someone were dividing a million and he was only offered one fourth of it. Other members of the group thought he was crazy, but he continued to reiterate that it was the principle that was important.

Another group of executives who knew each other well and didn't want to offend each other made several first divisions of 50-50 After a couple plays at the ultimatum game, several first proposers took advantage of their position and offered 55-45. They seemed to be saying that they had power and they were going to exercise it, but they weren't going to abuse it by taking a lot. Most of these proposals were accepted and, when they were recorded for everyone to see, reactions were mild. The proposals had seemed reasonable to most people.

When someone proposed 51-49, however, there were catcalls and loud "Ooooooohs" from the crowd. What was happening here? Why would this offer raise a reaction when 55-45 didn't? Rather than just taking advantage as the other offers had, the 51-49 proposal was perceived as a real put-down. It's almost as if the person said, "I'm better than you and I'm going to rub it in." Not surprisingly, this proposal was rejected.

The reactions to 55-45 and 51-49 proposals are unusual. From a psychological, personal point of view, however, especially in a group of competitive, status-conscious executives, the reactions are easily understandable.

Although economics clearly drives a significant portion of human behavior, how we react to each other depends on much more than expected economic outcomes and fiscal exchange. People usually have an ingrained sense of fairness; when someone else has treated you unfairly, you shy away from that person if you can.

Let's return to Pat's demand for $80,000. Was it fair? She proposed an unequal division of the money, but she provided a compelling reason. Thus, although Pat is demanding much more of the money, she isn't necessarily being unfair. How fair it might ultimately be we leave to the chapter on ethics. At the moment, we shift to an extension of the Ultimatum Game.

THE TWO-STAGE ULTIMATUM GAME

The Two-Stage Ultimatum Game extends the play an additional step. Now the second person can reject the first division and the bargaining is not over. Instead, after rejecting the first proposal, the second person divides a *reduced* amount of money. Let's say that the players start by dividing $100 and the second player rejects the first player's offer. She then proposes a division of less than $100, say $70. If the original, first proposer rejects the second offer, the game is over and both players get nothing. Or the first proposer can accept and the two will share $70. The big change in this game for the first proposer is knowing that the second person controls $70 on the second round. It's as if a disagreement is costly to both sides (as it is in labor-management negotiations) and the potential profits reflect this loss.

There are now three possible outcomes: (1) divide the money as the first person proposes (meaning the second person accepts the first offer); (2) divide the reduced amount of money as the second person proposes (meaning that the second person rejected the first division and the first person accepts the second division); or (3) both get nothing (meaning they both rejected each other's proposals).

In the Two-Stage Ultimatum Game, the shoe often changes feet: When the second round amount is high, the second person has a real advantage. Assume that you get to make the first division of $100 and that your offer is rejected. This means that you give control to the other person. She knows that she has control of $70, even as she responds to your first proposal. Thus, your first offer has to be good enough to tempt the second person to accept it and relinquish control of the $70.

Let's say that the second person is planning to split the $70 equally and expects that you would accept a $35-$35 split. That means that you must offer at least $35 to tempt her to accept your offer.

But what if, instead of an equal split, she is likely to offer you only $10 of the $70? If you were thinking of offering 50-50, you're in trouble. In the basic, one-stage Ultimatum Game, she would almost certainly accept the offer of an equal split. But now, she has the option of rejecting it and controlling the final take-it-or-leave-it offer. If she expects you to be economically rational (that is, you will take her offer, even if it is only $10), your first offer will have to give her more than a 50-50 split.

If you *knew* what she would do with the $70, you would have a better idea of what to do with your first offer. If you think that she's very rational and you offer her $70 of the initial $100, you can be pretty sure you will get $30. But can you do better?

If you ask for more than 50-50, you may be looking for problems: You indicate that you think an unequal division is okay, and you invite her to reject your offer and propose an unequal division that's much worse for you (for example, $55-$15, where you get only $15).

So you should probably offer at least 50-50. You can argue that it is fair, but the difficulty is that "fairness" is now self-serving; she may wonder whether you are using the 50-50, equal-split idea as a convenient argument. 50-50 in the basic Ultimatum Game was quite generous to the second person; in the Two-Stage Ultimatum Game, it is quite generous to the *first* person.

If we consider a different game where she would divide $90 in the second round, she would have even more control. But a 50-50 first offer is still plausible; it's prominent, it's equal, and you can argue that it's fair. But it gets increasingly risky as the amount of money that's available in the second round increases.

When this amount gets smaller, the Two-Stage Ultimatum Game looks like the one-stage game. If the costs of a disagreement are so high that the second person can only divide $10, her control plummets—but it doesn't disappear completely. She has at least as much control as she had in the basic Ultimatum Game when she could refuse an unfair proposal.

Another option for first dividers in the Two-Stage Ultimatum Game is to add a threat: "I won't accept anything you offer on the second round, regardless of what it is." Now the second person must either disbelieve the threat or accept the first offer. How credible is the threat? If the first person is rational and this is a one-time-only interaction, then the threat is not believable, because a valuable second offer is better than nothing. The economics of rationality indicate that this threat should *not* be credible—but for some, it can be successful.

The most stunning indication that economic theory doesn't work in ultimatum games occurs after a rejection. Most second proposers ask for *less* than they were originally offered. A second player might reject a $60-$40 division of the $100 and then only demand $35-35. If that happened only occasionally, we might think it was temporary insanity or just a stupid mistake. But in several recent studies, over 80 percent of the initial rejections were followed by these disadvantageous counterproposals. Economically, that makes no sense at all—why not just take the $40? But if feelings of fairness are important, it is completely sensible; second dividers tell firsts not only that they won't accept such a disproportionate, unfair division, but that they will also demand only a fair, equal split themselves. Sometimes principles of fairness supersede the logic of economics.

Most second proposals, though, offer an unequal division. It's almost as if second players have expected the first person to divide things fairly, have rejected the offer when he didn't, and have acted punitively by asking for more when they divide what's left. But even when the new division is close to being equal, it is sometimes rejected.

These funny behavior patterns suggest that the two players may be viewing the games quite differently. One may be playing a game of economics (the first person), the other a game of fairness (the second). Not surprisingly, their approaches match their individual interests. However, these different definitions of the situation can be mutually self-defeating when neither is willing to accept the other's expectations in the game. Putting yourself in the other person's shoes and understanding the reasons for his choices has tremendous strategic advantages in ultimatum games.

LABOR VERSUS MANAGEMENT

When you're buying a car from a dealer and you walk out before you reach an agreement, you are giving the dealer an ultimatum. If the dealer calls you back, he must come closer to accepting your last offer. When a company that has offered you a job says that the salary can't be increased any further, they are also making an ultimatum. The most frequent and pervasive examples of ultimatums, however, are the offers everyone receives to buy something through the mail. They usually include a stipulation saying, "If you don't buy before May 1, this offer will no longer be available. So act now!" Though we rarely hear the exact words "take it or leave it," that is the thrust in each case. These offers are strategic approaches to delivering ultimatums. When people are faced with a take-it-or-leave-it offer, it's easier for them to not think of it as an ultimatum. Especially if we hope that they will accept it.

Ultimatums are frequent, however, in labor-management negotiations, especially late in the negotiations (at "the eleventh hour") where they carry considerable force. These *commitments,* as they're called in collective bargaining, are one of the last cards either or both sides will play. They can make or break a tough negotiation.

When negotiations begin, labor and management often take strong opening stands. Management bemoans the fact that they can't offer the union very much, even though they would like to. The union bemoans the fact that they haven't gotten much from past contracts and that they need a lot more this time. Both sides try to position themselves so that they can ask for a lot and only concede when they must.

Concessions are necessary. As I've mentioned earlier, an old norm in bargaining, especially collective bargaining, is reciprocity. When one side makes a concession, the other side is expected to make a comparable concession. Quid pro quo is the way to go. Both sides may discount the concessions that the other side makes, arguing that they really aren't that important. At the same time, they both try to flatter themselves that they are the only side making really significant concessions.

Both sides always keep their eyes and ears open for indications of the other side's true preferences. They are constantly trying to ascertain each other's resistance points—the worst outcome either side would still accept before taking a strike. If management can discover that the union would be just barely satisfied with a 5-percent pay increase, then they will offer little more than that. Similarly, if labor discovers that management would grant an 8-percent pay increase but nothing more, they will typically push for just less than that. Clearly, information about the other's resistance point is incredibly valuable.

As information accumulates during the bargaining, one side may decide that they know enough to make an ultimatum. The head labor negotiator might then say, "We must have the seven-and-one-half-percent wage package or we are prepared to strike." This commitment is threatening, it's clear, and it's final, with no option apparent for the company but to accept the demand or suffer a strike. It looks like take-it-or-leave-it time, and labor has beaten management to the punch.

The language of collective bargaining, however, is subtle. Every word is important. Thus, when the union negotiator says, "We are prepared to. . . ," it does not mean that they *will* strike. Being prepared to strike and actually striking are two very different things.

Nevertheless, by presenting this commitment the union would like to convince management that this is a take-it-or-leave-it, last-chance, no-tomorrow ultimatum. If time is short, if they have accurately gauged what management can accept, and if their commitment is convincing, then their strategy will probably be successful. But three ifs make this commitment shaky, especially since the management team may analyze the union's exact words just as we have analyzed them here.

So what happens? Rather than caving in, management may refuse to comply. They may act as if the commitment was never made and simply proceed as if they never heard it. Or they may present a commitment of their own. Since the union negotiator won't like any of these responses, he may have decided to become unreachable right after he made the commitment. He may hide out until the other side has only enough time left to either accept the offer or hit the deadline, with its implicit threat of nonagreement and strike. Disappearing makes commitments more effective, and more risky.

Usually neither side wants an agreement before the eleventh hour. Anything before then might lead their constituents, the union members or the executives and stockholders of the firm, to think that they didn't bargain hard enough. Also, making a commitment too early leaves open too many opportunities for it to lose its impact. Thus, an effective commitment must be made late in the game, so that negotiations can only begin again with little time left before the deadline.

This looks like a very dangerous game (more on that in the next chapter). Both sides thrust and parry and delay and delay and delay until time is very tight and the chances of reaching an agreement seem to dwindle. The beauty of this process is that both sides typically know how the game is played and know to expect many of the seemingly dangerous twists of the negotiation process. In some sense, collective bargaining is like a Beethoven symphony: There are periods of calm and thunder followed by a climactic crescendo, exhilarating for both audience and performers. The players know the game and expect each other to play it well. The final interpretation and outcome of the symphony, and the negotiation, are somewhat in doubt and this makes the entire endeavor that much more compelling.

In the end, both sides must usually return to the bargaining table. They will do whatever they can to avoid caving in; the committed side will try to convince the other side that they have no alternative. The costs of a strike, to both sides, make these negotiations so dangerous. A misstep by either side might lead to an unnecessary strike—and missing an agreement that both prefer. (Sometimes a strike is inevitable, but that is unusual.)

To move a negotiator away from a commitment, the other negotiator typically has to make a commitment, too. That sets up a classic Game of Chicken (see Chapter 7): Both sides are committed to their course of action and hope that the other side will flinch first.

Negotiators who have made commitments and have also preserved an escape route for themselves, so that they don't get trapped with an untenable commitment, often do put the escape route into effect. They try to gracefully back away from their commitment and imply that the other side must make a similar, major concession.

THE DEADLINE

An important aspect of the collective bargaining process is the deadline. If bargainers were compelled to stick to the exact time when the contract expired, the collective bargaining process might have evolved differently. Instead, the games of commitment and ultimatum and push and pull that negotiators now play would have to occur earlier and, indeed, an entirely different process might be necessary. But as things stand, the apparent urgency of a fixed deadline is actually not terminal, since the deadline is rarely fixed.

Instead, final agreements can go somewhat beyond the typical midnight deadline. In many negotiations, the parties simply ignore the exact time. In others, their watches conveniently "stop working"—simultaneously. If the parties are experienced and see that an agreement is possible, an agreement will almost always happen. Both sides can publicly announce that they gave up a lot to get it; they can tell their constituents that they pushed the other side as far as they possibly could, even beyond the actual deadline.

Thus, ultimatums and last-second, deadline bargaining have become an integral part of labor-management negotiations. They reflect the fact that many issues in labor-management negotiations are *distributive*—they involve truly competitive issues where management and labor's interests are diametrically opposed. Labor wants the highest wages possible (within reason); management wants low wages to preserve profits for its stockholders. But they still have to live and work together for the length of the contract, and possibly of many contracts. Thus, even when one side has a supreme advantage (for various economic or organizational reasons), they will only push it gently.

If we return to Pat's demand for $80,000, the effects of the deadline and the likelihood of future contact might also be very important. If the first 2½ or 2¾ minutes disappear and Pat hasn't budged, you might get the idea that she really isn't going to come down at all. Certainly it would pay to wait as long as possible to see whether she would. But if she doesn't, what can you do? You must either concede to her ultimatum or refuse and have both of you get no money.

With respect to future interaction, would Pat's manners—she is warm, friendly, and polite while still standing firm—affect you? After it's all over and you conceded, it might make it easier for you to say that you did what any friend would. You do not have to explain that you were beaten. Indeed, the concept of winning and losing might only interfere with both of you gaining a significant sum of money. In essence, anything that Pat can do to provide you with a reasonable, acceptable explanation will help you concede. By being pleasant to bargain with, she may have increased her chances of getting $80,000.

OUTRAGEOUS ULTIMATUMS

Each collective bargaining situation is unique. The participants change, the company and the union change, the time changes, the locale changes. We have a wealth of stories and anecdotes about them, but we don't have a lot of control over what goes on, when, or why.

This is why experiments are so handy. We can repeat the same situation many times, without changing much, and see what happens.

Although most recent research on ultimatum games has been conducted by experimental economists, Gerald Leventhal, a social psychologist, experimented with similar phenomena some time ago. Two of his studies are particularly interesting. The first gave two people a simple task that each could observe the other doing. When they finished, the experimenter checked their performance, told them that they had both performed equally well, and then asked one of the two to divide their joint payoff of $2 (not very much, but a dollar was worth quite a bit more then). If the second person didn't like the first division, she could redistribute as much as 70 cents. Thus, the participants in this experiment were playing a Two-Stage Ultimatum Game. The first person was actually a colleague of the experimenter. Half the time he took $1.40 and gave the other person 60 cents; the other half of the time he took 60 cents and gave the other person $1.40.

Most of the people in this experiment did some redistributing. People who had originally been offered 60 cents shifted an average of 43 cents to themselves, giving them an average outcome of just over $1. They took just enough to make themselves equal, and a little more, almost as if they were penalizing the first person for implying that they weren't equal.

People who had originally been offered $1.40 also shifted an average of 43 cents! That gave the other person just more than a dollar and was a small self-sacrifice. On average, people refused to be overcompensated. They gave enough back to signify that the other person had been too magnanimous. Also, the final distributions in both cases were very close to dividing the two dollars equally, a dollar each.

Other conditions were also included in the study. Here the division was determined by a lottery, not by the other person. Those who received 60 cents redistributed, on average, about as much as before—this time 42 cents. However, overcompensated people (who got $1.40) only redistributed an average of 17 cents. When the face of fortune shines (and it's not some other person doing you a favor), people apparently are happy to keep more than they deserve.

This study and several others have indicated that people tolerate overcompensation more easily than undercompensation. When we're overcompensated, we may redistribute some of our winnings/earnings so that others with equal claims are not so undercompensated. But we may not respond as forcefully as when we're undercompensated. Not getting our fair share is much more energizing than getting more than our fair share.

Leventhal and his colleagues' second study investigated just how inequitable a payoff can be. This time, the participants had two opportunities to divide their payoffs after they completed two similar tasks. The real participant in the research divided a total of $1.20 after they completed the first task; the experimenter's colleague divided $1.40 after they completed the second. As expected, almost all (126 of 133) of the real subjects divided the money equally, with each getting 60 cents.

After finishing the second task, however, the experimenter's colleagues divided the money so that they received either $1.00 or $1.35 (of the total of $1.40)! Half the time they made this division matter-of-factly. The other half of the time, they behaved outrageously, saying, "I'm dividing the money this way because I'm so much better than you. Here's five cents [or forty cents] if you really want to take it."

Here we find an inequity ($1 versus 40 cents or a very inequitable $1.35 versus 5 cents) accompanied by either no explanation or an insulting, demeaning explanation. That put the recipients in a real bind since they could no longer redistribute 70 cents: In this study, they could only move 5 cents from one person to another.

Most people simply took the extra nickel. Of the people who got 5 cents and no insult, however, nine out of forty gave the nickel back; of the forty people who were also insulted, fifteen gave it back. In all, 30 percent of the people who received only 5 cents gave it back. Almost everyone who hears about this study says they would give the nickel back, too—if they thought of doing it at the time. (It's probably a prominent solution.) Most people's emotions are so strong, though, that they just don't see this option. Fortunately, the experimenters did not give people actual cash. Several people might have *flung* their nickel back.

CONCLUSIONS

Many situations lead to perceptions of inequity. "Overworked and underpaid" is a chronic condition for people who work. The reasons that drive these perceptions are important. People have a sense of fairness that determines whether they feel equitably treated. Frequently, the basis for their feelings of fairness is subtly determined by their own best outcomes. Thus, people who were poor, young liberals and now find themselves part of the prosperous middle class may find it hard to resist the tug of a more conservative political philosophy. Their ideas of what's fair change with their own condition.

In addition, when it comes to work, we tend to value what we do more than other people do. For a long time, I claimed that I never cooked anything that didn't taste great. Although I can't claim that anymore (due to some recent, disastrous culinary experiments), the fact that I could *ever* make that statement said more about my values than it did about my cooking. We like what we do. We like what we cook. If we like ourselves, we like the things that are associated with us.

The same is true about our jobs. We value our inputs, probably more than anybody else does. If we did it, it must be good. Thus, since others can't ever recognize how important our contributions are, they won't ever be rewarding us sufficiently. If they do, it's usually only short-lived—we acclimate to riches (and overcompensation) very rapidly. As a result, "overworked and underpaid" is very difficult—maybe impossible—to permanently eradicate.

Let's finally return to Pat's $80,000 demand. Have you decided what you would do if it came down to the last second? Would you take the $20,000? Would you demand $50,000 and refuse to concede?

If you had more time, you could project yourself, and Pat, into the future. Imagining the ultimate outcomes of your different strategic choices can make the selection of one of those strategies easier. You wouldn't have time to do this if you were actually in this situation and had to make the choice. You would also be emotionally caught up in the situation, so that cool, calm analysis would be difficult. But doing so here doesn't lose us anything, and it might be illuminating.

Let's restrict your strategic choices to make the analysis easier. You could (1) demand $50,000 and not settle for less; (2) accept the $20,000; or (3) try for the $50,000 and fall back to accepting the $20,000 if time is about to expire and Pat doesn't flinch. Thus, you will end up with either $50,000, $20,000, or nothing.

What happens after your decision may determine whether you feel happy about it later. Given either of the first two strategies, where you get at least some of the money, how would you feel if Pat's mother had the operation and totally recovered? You could congratulate yourself and tell your story for many years. What if, instead, Pat's mother died during the operation? Would you feel that the money was wasted? Would you congratulate yourself anyway and say that this is what you had to do?

Clearly, knowing that this might happen could change how you feel. If you could figure these things out in advance, it might change your strategy, too.

What if you took the $20,000 and Pat's mother recovered before the operation? Would you wait for her to give you $30,000 to make things even? Would you go and demand it? How would you resolve it? This could be pretty sticky. Although it would be wonderful for Pat's mother, it would mean a real problem for you. It might even make you wonder how sick her mother really was, and whether Pat had put one over on you.

What if, instead, Pat's mother died before the operation? Here you wouldn't have the doubts you had with the last possibility, but the difficulty with dealing with Pat afterward might be compounded by the grief she would be feeling. Grubbing for money, even a lot of money that you feel you deserve, from someone whose mother has just died is not a pretty prospect.

Finally, what if you gave in and then never heard from or saw Pat again? Man, oh man. Anger would probably be bubbling over, both toward Pat and toward yourself for getting suckered. That is your worst possible outcome. Trying to avoid it would certainly affect how you reacted to Pat's initial demand. Yet it's only one of five plausible outcomes to the situation.

What if? What if? We could consider other possibilities, but they are probably not really critical. The issues are clear: What comes after can determine your interpretation of what has happened before. Thus, it's worthwhile to project yourself into the future to see how you will feel given all the various possibilities. Even if you don't have time to do that in this situation, it's an exercise that can be very valuable in many situations.

What it means in the end is that several outcomes could transpire, and you have to be happy with your decision. You have several alternatives to consider. The final question remains: What would you do? There are no right answers to that question. It's an ultimatum that puts people to the test, as ultimatums often do. It's something that everyone can ponder. What's truly startling is the diversity of people's responses. Some people would take the $20,000 and be happy about it; some would take it but feel bitter. Others insist that they would not settle for less than $50,000, even if it meant the real risk of getting nothing.

Ultimatum games are truly basic. They're the ultimate stage in many negotiations. People react to them in many different ways, emphasizing once again how important it is to know yourself and your bargaining opponents.

CHAPTER 7

THE GAME OF CHICKEN

Smith and Company manufactures irrigation equipment and has just announced that they will be introducing a new pumping device that will increase efficiency. They have chosen one of three possible formats for the new system. They hope that their competitors will follow them and use the same format. Different formats will not easily accommodate each other (just as Beta and VHS VCRs and IBM and Apple computers are not very compatible).

When executives read about this case, they typically assume that Smith and the other companies in the market are playing the Game of Chicken. If new entrants use the same format as Smith's, they will concede a first-mover advantage to Smith but they'll all benefit from interchangeable equipment. If everyone chooses different formats, they all lose out as customers will be unwilling to invest in products that will restrict them to one producer. And, finally, if all of the new entrants use a format that's different from Smith's but the same as each others', they will be stuck in a serious, competitive battle that only one format might win (as has happened with VHS VCRs).

The Smith case is a business example of the Game of Chicken. The original game has a sad origin and some sad history. Teenagers in the 1950s played it, and sometimes died doing so. Thus, it is not a game to recommend, particularly in its original form.

Here's how it was played. Two guys took their cars to a lonely country road, usually at night. They often brought cheering sections that included friends and girlfriends. They sat with their cars facing each other, at some distance. The viewing audience was situated well back from the point where the cars would cross paths. Both drivers would start their cars and, on a prearranged signal, they would push the throttle to the floor and drive down the middle of the road directly at each other.

Each driver had two basic choices: to keep going straight or to turn and avoid a collision. If one went straight and the other turned off, the driver who kept driving down the middle and didn't flinch enhanced his reputation as someone who was really cool, really tough. The driver who turned off was called the Chicken.

If both drivers turned off and narrowly missed each other, both would win, at least a little: They showed their friends that they had enough courage to play the game and they let things go to the very last second. A couple scraped fenders made them both look even better—not as good as a guy who continued to go straight, of course, but pretty good.

The rub was if they both continued to go straight. When that happened, their reputations were probably enhanced: They would be remembered by some of their less discerning friends, at least for a little while, as really tough, really cool. But their lives would usually be over.

We can depict the drivers' choices and outcomes as we have before:

		Driver 2	
		Turn Off	Straight Ahead
	Turn Off	(2, 2)	(−2, 10)
Driver 1			
	Straight Ahead	(10, −2)	(death, death)

Again, the first outcome in each pair pertains to driver number 1, the second to driver 2. The numbers signify some measure of value, where more is better.

The Game of Chicken is a perfect example of what psychologist Paul Swingle called a "dangerous game," one that forces people to expose themselves to the risk of substantial loss when they threaten their opponent. Swingle used the example of small children accompanying their parents in public places as an everyday example of the Game of Chicken. Kids are quite adept at threatening to create a major disturbance while they simultaneously negotiate for favors. In the short term, it's better for the parent to be the Chicken and suffer the loss. In the long term, however, losses may accumulate and even escalate. At the same time, each time they play, the bothersome kid exposes himself to immediate punishment. It's dangerous.

Unlike the Gas Station and prisoner's dilemma games, both players in the Game of Chicken receive their worst outcomes simultaneously. The mutually noncooperative choice (driving straight ahead) now gives both players their very worst outcome.

In the example of Smith and Company, we can think of Smith driving the new pumping device down the road, prior to other companies revving up a similar product. When they do, they begin driving at each other, with Smith hoping that the others will flinch (and choose the same format that Smith is using). Smith has a clear first-mover advantage here. This also exists in other chicken games, as we'll see.

CREDIBLE THREATS

Another element that differentiates the Game of Chicken from prisoner's dilemma games is the potential for making effective threats. When both drivers discuss the rules they'll follow when they play the game (for example, if you turn away, make sure you turn to the *right*), they also have the opportunity to threaten each other. Both know that if they can convince the other driver that they definitely won't be turning away, the game will be much easier: They can drive straight without worry. Thus, Chicken is open to persuasion attempts via threats. Convincing the other driver to turn away is a worthwhile strategy—if it works. But that is a particularly huge if. The ultimate irony occurs when you feel that you have convinced the other driver to turn away and you are wrong.

What verbal threat is really credible in this situation? Would you trust your impressions when you think that you have scared the other driver into turning away? If you have scared him, why is he still playing the game? Clearly, most verbal threats are *not credible enough.*

What about nonverbal threats? You might scowl and act mean when you meet, just like professional boxers at a weigh-in. A fierce stare, in some situations, can be very frightening. Would it be memorable enough to convince someone to continue to play the game but turn away at the last moment? It sure is risky to think so.

What if you see a smile, a wicked smile, on the face of the other driver as he is driving toward you? Would that convince you to turn away? Of course, many of you may be saying to yourself that you wouldn't be foolish enough to play this game in the first place. But if you were a seventeen-year-old male with a hot car, how would you react to seeing grim determination or a devilish, demented smile on the other driver's face? Worse yet, if it was there and you didn't see it?

Strategically, you could never *depend* on the effectiveness of verbal or nonverbal threats. You couldn't be sure that your threat was credible enough or even that it was perceived accurately. You would still have a difficult choice when the time came.

A more effective but much more unusual message is one Herman Kahn outlined in his book, *On Escalation.* As the drivers are approaching each other and are in clear sight of one another, one driver throws his steering wheel out the window! Now we have a tremendously credible threat. Would you continue driving straight when you knew the other driver could no longer control the steering of his car?

This action provides considerable clarity to the situation. But what if *both* drivers thought about throwing their steering wheels out of their cars (also noted by Kahn)? What gives when one driver sees the other's wheel flying out his window when he has just removed his own steering wheel?

The Game of Chicken and some of the endgame dynamics of the Ultimatum Game are essentially the same. In labor-management negotiations, one side may present the other side with an ultimatum near the end of their deliberations. The threat offered by a driver in the Chicken Game who states verbally, in advance, that he won't turn away, and who waits until the very last second to turn, is exactly the same kind of act. It is meant to influence the other party to concede and thus reach an agreement that is valuable to the threatener.

One of the troubles with threats, however, is counterthreats. In labor-management negotiations, the side that makes a late threat would hate to discover that the other side is also about to respond in kind and there is no way to stop it. When both sides make threats, they make it harder for either to concede; to do so makes one lose face. When two people make simultaneous ultimatums, it may take a Chicken to back down and concede. No one wants to be the Chicken—but the alternative can be so much worse.

BLACKMAIL

The difficulty with making threats was nicely analyzed by Daniel Ellsberg, an economist who worked at the Rand Corporation in the 1950s and 1960s and became notorious for his activities in the peace movement in the 1970s, when he released the Pentagon Papers. His paper was provocatively titled *The Theory and Practice of Blackmail.*

Ellsberg showed that the real difficulty for blackmailers (or anyone using coercion) is to convince their potential victims that they will carry out their threat if the victim doesn't comply. Ellsberg tells several interesting stories, my favorite being one about an older woman who robbed banks. It seems that this frail-looking sexagenarian would walk into a bank, go up to the counter, produce a glass with some clear liquid in it, and pass a note to the teller. The note read: "Give me all the bills in your drawer." When the teller looked up, this sweet-looking woman would tilt the glass to make the liquid in it move. "See this," she would say. "It's acid. You wouldn't want it in your face, would you?"

If you were the teller, how would you react? This seemingly pleasant old lady is speaking quietly about acid in a glass, saying that she might throw it all over your face. Not something you'd even like to contemplate.

But wouldn't you wonder, "Is it really acid?" It looked like any clear liquid. It would have been very easy for her to simply put water in the glass. The basic issue, as it is with all threats, is whether her threat is *credible enough*. Bank tellers are told not to resist attempts at theft, especially if violence is threatened. The bank would rather have tellers take the Chicken role than get hurt. Tellers may be able to sound an alarm without being detected, but they should have little hesitation in handing over the money.

Actually, the little old lady's threat was credible enough. She was a successful bank robber, at least for a while. She was only holding a glass of water, but that doesn't really matter, since her threat was strong enough to be effective. It might not be credible enough in other situations. If she stopped you on the street and asked for your money, you might be tempted to simply duck and run. Changing the situation can change whether a threat is credible enough.

THE BLACKMAILER'S PARADOX

Blackmailers' threats generally involve a paradox: By punishing a victim who resists, they set themselves up for greater punishment. If a bank teller resisted and the little old lady actually threw acid in his face, she would have gone to jail for a much longer time than if she hadn't thrown any acid. If a bank teller resisted and she simply dropped everything and left the bank, she could still escape. And if she were caught, she would clearly be in trouble, but a lot less trouble.

This paradox is true for almost all threat and blackmail attempts. Following through with a threat is costly. Threats are truly successful only if they go unchallenged. Parents who carry out threats to their children stereotypically say that it hurts them more than it hurts the child. From the parent's point of view (not the child's), that may be true. Similarly, superpowers have to be very careful when they are dealing with Third World countries. Making a threat that you don't want to carry out is much worse than making no threat at all. Having to actually carry it out can be even worse. Similarly, big companies cannot be too cavalier in their negotiations with small companies. Again, threats may be simply too costly to fulfill, in terms of reputations and objective costs.

While a powerful party can threaten a weaker party, such threats are risky because they have so much status to lose. Even without status differences, however, threats are inherently problematic. They are almost always paradoxical. If the victim is aware of the Blackmailer's Paradox, it makes the threatener's task of establishing credibility that much more difficult. How then can a blackmailer make an essentially incredible threat credible?

REPUTATIONS

If a victim successfully resists, our little old lady bank robber loses some of her reputation. The story is bound to appear in the newspapers and other bank tellers will be alerted to the woman who really won't throw what might or might not be acid. So although a blackmailer may face less punishment if she does not follow through with her threat, she also loses some of her reputation. And reputations are extremely important in establishing the credibility of a threat—even for a blackmailer.

After news reports of her thwarted attempt at theft, our bank robber would now have to come up with a much more convincing threat to be credible on her next robbery attempt. Her original threat was credible enough when she first used it. Now that her reputation has been damaged, however, she needs to do more to be convincing.

You may ask whether she had any reputation at all when she began robbing banks. Well, she may not have needed much of a reputation before her first robbery attempt. The simple fact that she had enough nerve to go to a bank and attempt to rob it immediately establishes her reputation. This is much like the reputation Vito Corleone established for himself in the early moments of *The Godfather.* His lack of a reputation led Don Cicci to laugh at his proposal to be left alone. When he strengthened his position by following up with a tremendously daring, violent act, his reputation in the neighborhood was established. Early successes, well publicized, are tremendously important for blackmailers. Thus, when a report of our little old lady's first successful robbery reached the papers, her reputation was established. A failure diminished it quickly—reputations are particularly fragile—but they are very important, even for a blackmailer.

Another way to increase the credibility of a threat is to act irrationally as you make the threat. Bank tellers who are approached by a little old lady asking for money may respond by saying (or at least thinking), "What? Are you crazy?" But by asking that question, they can't help but respond in the affirmative. Anyone crazy enough to be robbing a bank may be crazy enough to follow through with a threat that hurts themselves as much or more than it hurts the victim. If you can appear a little mad . . .

The Game of Chicken, then, is ripe for threats. The difficulty with this game is that if you respond to a threat by conceding, you can do little in the future except respond to further threats with further concessions.

PLAYING THE GAME

The Game of Chicken puts people in a situation where there is no longer a clear short-term strategy (as there was in Chapter 4 in the Gas Station Game). In the battle for the VCR market, it wasn't clear at first whether the Beta or VHS format would win. The best short-term choices depend on knowing what to expect from the other player or from the market.

When I ask people to play the Game of Chicken, there is no need for anyone to die (as people did in the original game). Thus, I alter the original formulation somewhat. Instead of being two teenagers driving their cars at each other, the players are the presidents of two competing trucking companies. They can choose to send their trucks along normal routes or unusual routes. The unusual routes are winding, mountainous roads that cut down on travel time if there is little traffic. They are very unprofitable, however, if other trucking firms begin to use them. Normal routes entail less risk and typically lead to moderate financial returns.

The profits for the two firms, in hundreds of thousands of dollars, are shown below.

| | | The Other Firm | |
		Normal Route	Risky Route
You	Normal Route	(2, 2)	(−1, 6)
	Risky Route	(6, −1)	(−4, −4)

You and the other firm are both aware of the risky and normal routes. You both also know that you both know them. You cannot collude with each other since that's illegal. Thus, you both will make a series of simultaneous, secret choices. You find out soon after each choice whether the other firm has taken the risky or the normal route.

When people play this Chicken Game repeatedly, they react in one of several distinct ways. Some pairs both choose the normal route time after time. They reap a moderate reward but report that during the game, they are constantly tense because they are afraid that their opponent might switch to the risky route. Then they'll be in a quandary—should they suffer moderate losses for a long time or try to convince their opponent to change by inflicting large losses on both of them? Even when the two firms achieve mutual, long-term cooperation, they attribute it not so much to their own and their counterpart's moral character, but rather to the fact that they learned not to be competitive in the Gas Station Game.

Other people choose the normal route until one chooses the risky route. Then, there is often a long delay because the other party now finds itself on the horns of a terrible dilemma: Choose the risky route to demonstrate strength (but lose profits) or choose the normal route to lose less?

Most people choose the risky route; they are driven more by pride than by profits. They refuse to be considered weak and choose to pay additional (fictitious) costs (from $100,000 to $400,000) to avoid being labeled the Chicken (even though that label is never mentioned).

Several pairs begin by choosing the risky route. They are quite unusual and find that their subsequent negotiating time is spent trying to get out of the bind that almost inevitably develops. Stopping this mutually destructive inertia is very difficult, even though an independent shift to the normal route is self-beneficial. The problem is that such a shift is tremendously other-beneficial.

When players in this bind can talk to one another, they try to establish some basis for trust. Even though either can do better by switching to the normal route, the loss of face from letting the other do so well tends to outweigh one's own payoff gains. Both sides typically resolve the uncertainties they have about the other side by promising retaliation in the event of a double cross.

Groups make positive "threats" much less often. They rarely say that they will choose the normal route as long as their counterpart does. Instead, people present the exact same contingency as a negative, punishing threat: for instance, "I'll choose the risky route forever if you choose it even once." Both messages communicate a form of the Tit for Tat strategy, but the negative threat is used much more frequently. This might contribute to why people sometimes succumb to temptation, choosing the risky, competitive route as the deadline looms near.

Indeed, the end point makes the temptation to choose the risky route quite strong. Most players report that they were acutely aware of that temptation, but most were more worried about their counterpart's temptations than their own. Pairs that mutually resisted the temptation on the last trial simultaneously breathed a big sigh of relief when the final choices were posted.

STRATEGIES

Being the first to act competitively, and threatening never to change, puts a credible threatener in position to win the game. In the VCR battle, aggressive promotion of the VHS format may have turned the tide, even though the Beta format had technological advantages. When public opinion and public purchasing began to turn toward VHS, Beta lost ground slowly at first, and then very rapidly.

Although both parties in a Chicken Game have less incentive to choose noncooperatively (compared with the prisoner's dilemma), the payoffs encourage them to be the first to compete and threaten and hope that the threat is sufficiently credible to result in continued nonaggression by the other player.

Is the converse true? In other words, can one person unilaterally push the situation toward mutual cooperation? In prisoner's dilemma games, the Tit for Tat strategy reinforced others for choosing cooperatively and punished them for choosing noncooperatively. In the Game of Chicken, Tit for Tat may also work, but the costs are so much higher. Now if a move toward noncooperation by one leads to noncooperation by the other, they both get their worst outcomes. Both pay more if one competes and threatens and the other responds in kind, which is just like management and labor suffering a strike.

If the game lasts a long time, though, conceding to a threat can be much worse than counterthreatening. Succumbing to a blackmailer, for instance, may lead to greater threats in the future. The difficulty is that you must absorb an immediate cost if you counterthreaten. Thus, a player faced with a threat in a Chicken Game is faced with a real dilemma—two outcomes, both bad.

If you don't concede, you must match the threat with your own threat. If both sides follow through, both get their worst outcomes (death in the original Game of Chicken). When we take things to their logical conclusion, we ask the following question: "Is preserving your reputation worth dying for?"

When the mutually noncooperative outcome is not so devastating, counterthreats may be the only way to go. But you need to consider the costs you will incur, even in the short run. Expert threateners not only realize that they face a paradox, but that their victim will, too. Thus, a sequence of threat and counterthreat generates a nest of paradoxes. We shouldn't expect their resolution to be simple and easy.

It's now quite clear why Chicken is such a dangerous game. It's easy to see why teenagers should not play the original version. It's sometimes less clear in other situations. The bottom line, however, is that threats are dangerous all by themselves, since using them invites entry into a Game of Chicken. The only solution, and a relatively unlikely one, is for the original threatener to withdraw her threat.

Threats made in the heat of emotion may disappear over time, when the threatener's emotions have cooled and the motivation to enforce the threat disappears. Allowing someone to take back a threat and simultaneously save face represents a diplomatic triumph, for both parties.

Recipients can also ignore the fact that a threat has been communicated and effectively blunt the players' mutual entry into a Game of Chicken, as John F. Kennedy did when he ignored Khrushchev's formal letter during the Cuban missile crisis. This was one factor among many that helped the two countries back out of a Game of Chicken that threatened much of the world with its mutually noncooperative outcome. In the same fashion, ominous labor-management negotiations sometimes, at the brink of a mutually costly strike, lead to cooler heads and unexpected agreements.

Occasionally a Chicken Game will lead to one side taking

the risky choice and the other side finding that its best option is to simply accept it. Those situations are rare, but they arise when long-term outcomes are not affected much by the other person's threats, and short-term costs from a counterthreat are high. Even when such short-term costs for counterthreatening do exist, not responding in kind can ruin your reputation. To avoid that, you normally must counterthreaten.

An example of this situation is the response of the poor farmers in the movie *The Seven Samurai* (or the American version, *The Magnificent Seven*), who continually conceded to a group of bandits until the situation became completely unbearable. Finally, the farmers enlisted the aid of the seven samurai to counterthreaten the bandits, even though this meant an immediate increase in violent hostilities.

THREATS AND POWER

One important issue, not yet raised, is the power behind the threat. When someone with power makes a threat, most people listen. Threat credibility and power go hand in hand. The power of the counterthreatener, however, is also important. Consider the following three situations: (1) Two parties have little power over each other; (2) one party has considerably more power than the other; and (3) both parties have considerable power over each other.

Two different but reasonable lines of thought address these situations. *Bilateral deterrence,* a well-known theory in international politics, suggests that two parties are less likely to use their power as they increase their power over each other. They each increase their fear of the other and, therefore, refrain from attacking, or even threatening. This argument suggests that building more nuclear arms to keep pace with potential enemies is the best way to achieve peace.

Conflict spiral theory, which is well known in psychology, suggests just the opposite: Parties who increase their power over each other will be *more* likely to use that power, since having more power increases your temptation to attack. Also, when you see someone else's power increasing, you assume that their temptation to attack will be increasing, too. This argument suggests that peace is best achieved by disarmament.

Both approaches also address the dynamics of unequal power. On the one hand, bilateral deterrence suggests that parties with unequal power will use their force more than parties with equal power. The weaker of the two will expect attack more often; the stronger will fear retaliation less. Both feelings are conducive to greater attacks. Conflict spirals, on the other hand, predict that unequal power will reduce the use of power. The higher-power party feels that using power is unnecessary; the weaker party is also less tempted because it feels it won't be very effective.

Subscribing to bilateral deterrence would drive you to always want to increase your power capabilities, regardless of the actions of your opponents. Believing in conflict spirals should reduce your motivation to increase your power, also with little regard for what your opponent does. The approaches emphasize either fear of power or temptations to use it. Until recently, no one had even discussed the fact that these two reasonable theories are in direct conflict.

Early experimental research that addresses these theories for individuals (rather than the superpowers) has found that bargainers with different power capabilities used threats, especially when they didn't have much power. Unequal power led to more conflict. When both parties could seriously hurt each other, equal power led to less conflict. These results support the theory of bilateral deterrence: A buildup of individual strength reduced conflict when strength was equal, but unequal power increased conflict.

This principle may have been understood by the Spanish explorers during the conquests of Central and South America. Spanish troops had considerable advantages technologically and could overpower native tribes. But they were always outnumbered and could not afford to leave enough troops to retain control when they moved on. Folklore has it that they appointed two joint chiefs, with one having slightly more power than the other. The ensuing internal rivalry made it much easier for a few Spanish troops to retain control.

CONCLUSIONS

Chicken games are dangerous. Threats and counterthreats can push two people or two groups toward mutual destruction. The legendary feud of the Hatfields and the McCoys is a pertinent example. Once they began threatening and retaliating, they had real difficulties backing down. Generations later, family members didn't even know why the feuds had begun.

We see again how emotions come into play. Pride and loss of face can interfere with the more reasonable responses of backing down and retracting threats. Indeed, the conflict may escalate and lead to increasing costs for everyone concerned, even innocent bystanders.

In the end, when we consider that threats are only effective if they're not challenged, and that people who are threatened usually react emotionally and reciprocally, we realize that Chicken is a game to avoid—unless you are sure of the ultimate outcome. Threats are a negotiation strategy that is akin to walking into a meeting with a stick of dynamite that you've already lit. You will get your way in the bargaining some of the time, particularly when you're already powerful. But then you usually don't need the dynamite. If you do need it, you may have forced an interaction into a Game of Chicken, and you've increased your chances of getting burned—badly.

CHAPTER 8

THE BATTLE
OF THE SEXES

Most people equate bargaining and negotiation with competition. They are only partly right. Most bargaining games do include some competition; at the same time, however, every negotiation depends on an agreement, and a necessary part of any agreement is that people cooperate, at least a little.

Total competition is hard to find. Poker and war are often used as examples of games of complete competition. But neither really qualifies. Can you imagine playing poker with a group of people who are completely competitive throughout the game? Certainly playing the hands is competitive (if it isn't, it might mean that some of the players are cheating), but eating sandwiches, consuming drinks, smoking cigars, talking during play, and the joy people have from playing poker are rarely competitive. If they were, few people would play.

War is the other prototypical example of competition. Yet Robert Axelrod, in his excellent book *The Evolution of Cooperation,* tells the story of German and American troops fighting opposite one another in World War I. Although their commanders ordered them to fire on each other at various times, they often worked around the competition of war by making sure that they wouldn't kill anyone. Shots were consciously fired over the heads of the other side, and shellings were repeated in a systematic order, so that, before long, the opposing commander would know exactly where the next shells were going to hit. The life-or-death struggle that we associate with war, that is, as a strictly competitive bargaining game, doesn't fit this scenario.

THE TELEPHONE GAME

Unfortunately, completely cooperative games are also fairly rare. But a small town in Iowa provides a real-life example that we call the Telephone Game. The town's telephone system was very erratic; conversations frequently disconnected for no apparent reason. People then had to decide whether they should call back or wait for the person they were talking with to call back.

This is the very simplest type of bargaining game. It is totally cooperative. You both do well at the same time; you both do badly at the same time. One and only one of you must call back while the other waits. If you both call back, you'll both get a busy signal; if you both wait, you both wait.

When we split groups into callers and callees to play the Telephone Game, everyone must choose to call back or wait (simultaneously and without speaking with each other). The solution is actually pretty easy; most people get it right the first time. A few callers don't call back, though, and a few more callees do. Just like in Iowa, those who called originally were, for the most part, the ones who called back. The people in the Iowa town were understandably aggravated with the telephone system; they often complained. But they also solved their problem, without ever talking about it.

When we run the game a second time and switch roles (callers are now callees; callees are now callers), almost everyone gets it right. There are always, however, a few who don't, and they get very embarrassed. The third round of the game always leads to unanimous responses. It doesn't take long to learn the Telephone Game.

DEPENDENCE

The logic behind this solution is quite simple. The original caller must have had something in mind when he called. The original callee was simply the receiver of the call. Thus, the caller probably needed to complete the call more than the callee did. Since the caller gets more from reconnecting the call, he should expend more effort to reconnect it.

Another way of thinking about this interaction is to realize that the caller is *dependent* on the callee. The very act of calling indicates, at least in this short interaction, that the callee has more power in the situation than the caller. In bargaining that results in a deadlock, whoever makes the next offer may indicate that they need an agreement more. By doing so, they communicate their greater dependence, and because people don't want to seem dependent, this makes resolving deadlocks that much more difficult. People often put a lot of stock in waiting for the other side to make the first move. It's a power play that can interfere with agreements that would benefit both sides. The danger is that such an agreement is likely to favor the bargainer who is less dependent (that is, the person who doesn't really need the deal).

ANOTHER COORDINATION GAME

The Battle of the Sexes is a story that has been told often. I don't know exactly who originated or named it. For this discussion, I've altered the details, but the general thrust remains the same.

An older couple who lives in the country goes to the big city once every ten years. They can never afford to stay for more than just one night. They are so old now that they expect this trip to be their last. In previous years they had done different things on their night in town; they now have to decide where they will go for their last night in the city. They check into their favorite hotel, and decision time is upon them. Although they haven't decided, they have narrowed things down: They prefer to do something together rather than doing anything apart. In this sense, the Battle of the Sexes is like the Telephone Game. The problem is that their preferences are very different. Their choices and outcomes look like this:

		Husband's Preferences			
		Boxing Match	Blues Bar	Fancy Dinner	The Opera
Wife's Preferences	Boxing Match	4, 1	0, 0	0, 0	0, 0
	Blues Bar	0, 0	3, 2	0, 0	0, 0
	Fancy Dinner	0, 0	0, 0	2, 3	0, 0
	The Opera	0, 0	0, 0	0, 0	1, 4

(The first number in each pair is the wife's outcome; the second number is the husband's. All the numbers refer to rankings: 4 indicates the most preferred alternative, 0 the least.)

The wife prefers the boxing match to the blues bar, the bar to the fancy dinner and the dinner to the opera. The husband prefers the opera to the fancy dinner, the dinner to the blues bar and the bar to the boxing match. (Some people like to pause a minute here to visualize what this couple looks like.) How can they decide where to go?

SOLUTIONS

The Battle of the Sexes is intriguingly but unfortunately named. *Anyone* can have a conflict like this. These people would like to cooperate and go to the same event together; at the same time, they may compete over which event to attend. It is a classic case of mixed motives (cooperation and competition). Partners and businesses often face the same problem when they agree on the ends but differ on the means (as we will see with an example later in this chapter).

Many people assume that the husband and wife will compromise. But how? They might eliminate the boxing match and the opera but they still have to choose between the blues bar and the fancy dinner. (We assume that they only have time or energy for one of the two; they can't do both.) In previous years they could resolve the problem by saying, "You can have your choice this year if I can have mine ten years from now." But they can't do that now.

Hardheaded solutions to this conflict are the opposite of compromise; they suggest that one person be totally stubborn. The wife, for instance, might say, "Alright, I know how you feel about things. I don't know what you're going to do, but I'm going to the boxing match. 'Bye." Then she abruptly leaves the hotel room and heads for the boxing arena. If she can pull this off effectively, what can the husband do? He can go to any of the other places, but his payoff would be 0 because he prefers to attend any of the events *with* his wife rather than going somewhere alone. (At least he did when they first arrived.) She has truncated his choices so that he must choose from the first row of payoffs, where the boxing match's outcome of 1 is better than anyplace else. If he is particularly rational, he should simply trundle off to the boxing match and enjoy it and his wife's company as much as he can—and ignore the fact that he is at his least preferred event and she is at her most preferred. By being stubborn, the wife has been able to go to her most preferred event.

This strategy, however, pays little attention to the fact that the husband may not be particularly rational, and that our couple must make a long drive home together in close proximity in the same car and live in the same house. The ill feelings generated by the stubborn wife may come back to haunt her (or both of them). A more realistic approach might be one that (1) looks for additional alternatives or (2) even removes some of the available alternatives.

The second of these two options is easy. They might arrive in town and find that tickets for the boxing match or the opera are not available, that the fancy restaurànt is full, or that the blues bar is holding a benefit rock-and-roll concert (something that neither of them want to see). If none of their four options were available, they would truly be out of luck and would have to come up with other alternatives. If three of the alternatives were unavailable, their choice would be easy: They could simply go to the one that was left. If two were not possible, they would have the same problem they began with, although with fewer alternatives. Their conflict might be just as intense. If only one of the alternatives were unavailable, they could compromise.

Another way to solve their problem is to generate an additional alternative. If, after their arrival, the husband buys the local newspaper to check out what's happening in town and discovers that a modern dance company is performing that evening, would that help? It will if this new alternative is not a top preference for the wife. Let's assume it's in third place for both of them:

		Husband's Preferences				
		Boxing Match	Blues Bar	Modern Dance	Fancy Dinner	The Opera
	Boxing Match	5, 1	0, 0	0, 0	0, 0	0, 0
	Blues Bar	0, 0	4, 2	0, 0	0, 0	0, 0
Wife's Preferences	Modern Dance	0, 0	0, 0	3, 3	0, 0	0, 0
	Fancy Dinner	0, 0	0, 0	0, 0	2, 4	0, 0
	The Opera	0, 0	0, 0	0, 0	0, 0	1, 5

This should solve everything. The new alternative is an easy compromise: Both give up their first two choices; neither has to suffer either of their last two choices.

The difficulty here is that the husband came up with the new idea. When one of two "competing" parties generates a new alternative, the other may wonder whether something fishy is going on. The possibility of ulterior motives may rear its ugly head, possibly leading the wife to speculate, "I bet modern dance is actually his first choice, not his third. Modern dance is much more like going to the opera or a fancy dinner than going to a boxing match or a blues bar. I'll be damned if I let him get away with this." So what might look like a simple solution to the problem may not be, even if the husband were totally honest and upfront about the whole situation.

THE VALUE OF A MEDIATOR

The principle of adding an alternative when you are deadlocked is still a good way to resolve conflict. It just has to be executed *in a different way* than we've just described. Consider this change: Instead of the husband checking the newspaper, we find the couple in the lobby of their hotel, relaxing over a drink and discussing what they will do that evening. They go to the concierge and ask about tickets to the boxing match and the opera, reservations at the restaurant, and who is playing at the blues bar. She tells them that all of the alternatives are available and that their choices are excellent. At the same time a perceptive concierge might realize that they are having a hard time deciding where to go. She suggests that they might also consider the modern dance performance that night. Now the couple's discussion is no longer tainted by the possibility of ulterior motives; an impartial third party has suggested a new alternative and the resolution of their dispute can proceed as we hoped it would when we began the story.

The role of a third party in this situation is critical. She can act as a mediator who is only interested in helping the parties resolve the conflict; she has no other interests in the battle. Mediators are often very effective in collective bargaining disputes, community disputes, divorce negotiations, and as intermediaries in what might otherwise develop into adversarial courtroom confrontation.

Mediators work best by acting as a buffer and removing the personal attributions that the combatants might otherwise make about each other. They can say to each of the two parties; "The other side would probably be very receptive to this new idea." Both parties can believe the content of the message without the uncertainties that would come with the same message if it came from the mouth of the other party. In addition, neither party has to take the first step in making a concession; the mediator can do it for them. Mediators can probe for possible agreements without revealing whether the idea came from one of the disputants. In doing so, neither side has to admit any weakness to the other party.

But mediators typically have limited power. They are usually invited to a dispute and can only make suggestions to the parties. The concierge works well as a mediator in this example but in other, less personal impasses, procedures like arbitration may be needed, since they provide third parties with additional power.

ARBITRATION

Arbitrators, like mediators, are expected to be impartial (although that is an ideal that is only occasionally achieved). Arbitrators listen to both sides and, in the end, make a decision that ends the conflict. When arbitration is binding, both sides agree in advance to abide by the decision. (When it is not binding, arbitrators have no more power than mediators.)

Many public sector groups (for example, the police, nurses, city workers, teachers) resolve their collective bargaining conflicts via compulsory arbitration; they hire an arbitrator when they can no longer make any progress by themselves. In doing so, they lose control of the decision-making process. As a result, both sides try to avoid arbitration, not only because of the loss of control but also because of the uncertainty it generates. Who knows how an arbitrator will ultimately rule? Even when people are very confident that their position is totally fair and completely reasonable—and this is normal for most people—relinquishing control means some uncertainty. To avoid it, people try to negotiate an agreement without help. That way they can also establish a tradition of working together.

Conventional and *final offer* are the most common forms of arbitration. In conventional arbitration, the arbitrator listens to both sides, solicits the groups' final positions, and can impose an agreement anywhere between them. The difficulty is that conventional arbitration can encourage the parties to avoid serious negotiations. Conventional arbitration rewards both parties for being tough. By coming out strong and being inflexible, the parties can avoid conceding and looking weak. In addition, if an arbitrator is going to split the difference between the disputants' final offers, then staking a final position as far as possible from the other party's is the thing to do. Thus, conventional arbitration can have what's called a *chilling effect* on negotiations: Both parties are encouraged to be *cool* to bargaining seriously.

Final offer arbitration, on the other hand, encourages the parties to get down to serious bargaining and get as close to an agreement as they can. If they can't negotiate an agreement by themselves, they submit final offers to an arbitrator, who must choose one of them and can no longer split the difference. Knowing that the most reasonable final offer will have the best chance, both parties are more likely to negotiate in earnest. Bargainers who avoid making concessions are left with little information about the other party and little idea about what would be an effective final offer. To avoid this, they tend to be much more active, conscientious negotiators. Fewer disputes have to be arbitrated; the parties keep control of their own conflict; and they often find that if they do have to make final offers, they both concede enough to reach an agreement without needing the arbitrator.

Major league baseball settles salary disputes with final offer arbitration. When an experienced player and his team cannot agree to terms, the two sides submit their final offers to an arbitrator. They also present arguments to support their case: That causes players to accentuate their positives and owners to emphasize their limitations. Knowing this, several teams work hard to avoid arbitration; they don't want to attack their own players, even in private. Thus, some teams are proud that they have never gone to arbitration. As you might expect, though, these teams probably pay higher salaries when they finally agree. By committing themselves to reaching a negotiated agreement, they give the player a strong bargaining position. Indeed, most of these agreements come very close to the player's final demands.

INTRAVENTION

Both mediation and arbitration are formal third party mechanisms. But many disputes also include third parties in less formal ways.

Recently I coined the term *intravention* to refer to the actions of informal third parties who are usually members of the same organization as the disputants and have power over them (for example, their manager or immediate superior). Unlike the term *inter*vention, which indicates that a third party comes between two disputants, *intra*vention denotes that informal third parties often come from within the organization and, in addition, have the power to terminate the dispute. They may also have (1) personal interests that are affected by the dispute or (2) stronger positive feelings toward one disputant or the other.

Consider an example: When two employees can't stand each other, it may be difficult for them to get any work done. Their supervisor might intravene and mildly suggest that they get on with the job. The implications of this directive are pretty obvious.

A similar example: Siblings are particularly adept at aggravating one another, especially when they are on a long trip. Their parents then have to act as the family's internal security force; they intravene to preserve their sanity during what they hoped would be a vacation.

Both of these examples show how the intravention of a strong third party is both necessary and frequent in typical, everyday groups. Avoiding conflict often requires a third party; a third party with power should be particularly effective. Not surprisingly, third parties with intravention power tend to use it by imposing an agreement, possibly after they have tried to mediate first.

PERSUASION

Third parties can be very helpful, especially in formal interactions like those in the business world. They can introduce a new alternative; they can make the final decision after considering the disputants' final offers; they can sometimes impose a solution. All these outcomes resolve the conflict. But if we return to our old couple in the city, we might wonder whether they can do anything short of involving a third party to resolve their conflict easily. People's preferences often differ. Maybe there is a simpler way.

Persuasion might be the simplest solution. If the husband and wife in our story have warm, positive feelings for each other, they will want to resolve their disagreement as easily as they can, without serious conflict. At the same time, however, they may really want to see the opera or the boxing match. A convincing, persuasive argument is almost costless and generally provides both people with a positive outcome. But influencing someone to change her preferences to yours, when it's clear that you are simply arguing on your own behalf, is very difficult. The other person typically thinks that you are arguing only to get your own way, which may be no better for her than several other alternatives. Once one person suspects ulterior motives on the part of the other, effective resolution of the conflict becomes more difficult. And once we think ulterior motives exist, we rarely forget them. Thus, persuasion is a strategy that is very difficult to implement effectively.

On the other hand, friendship often means that persuasion

is not necessary. You gain when a friend benefits. Thus, some couples get into arguments because each wants to go to the *other's* most preferred event. Several years ago I visited some friends who were in the midst of buying their first house. They had seen three acceptable houses and were trying to decide which to bid on. Paul had clear preferences, but Jane had a hard time making up her mind. Paul steadfastly refused to reveal his preferences; he knew that, if he did, Jane would simply agree. So, instead, he tugged and pulled and pushed her—for well over an hour—to express a preference. Finally she expressed the slightest of preferences, which just happened to be the house he liked best, too. We might think of this interaction as reverse persuasion. It's a lot like my negotiation for the electric broom with my friend Lou, described in the first chapter.

STRENGTH OF PREFERENCE

Especially when one person has much stronger feelings than the other, it might make sense to let him have his way. Let's assume, then, that the wife of the older couple we left in the city is almost indifferent to all of the possible alternatives and that the husband has very, very strong preferences for the opera. Going to any of the four choices together is far preferable to her to going anywhere alone; the same is true for him, but all of his intensity centers on the opera. Now their preferences might look like the chart on page 151.

While the ranking of their preferences is the same as before, it's now clear that if we can add the couple's ratings for each of the alternatives, the opera wins easily. The husband wants it so much more than the other alternatives, and the wife wants it only slightly less. Its total of 13 far outdistances the equal totals of 7 for the other three alternatives. The couple will easily maximize their joint outcome by going to the opera.

People who are friends usually deal easily with issues like

| | | Husband's Preference | | | |
		Boxing Match	Blues Bar	Fancy Dinner	The Opera
	Boxing Match	6, 1	0, 0	0, 0	0, 0
Wife's Preference	Blues Bar	0, 0	5, 2	0, 0	0, 0
	Fancy Dinner	0, 0	0, 0	4, 3	0, 0
	The Opera	0, 0	0, 0	0, 0	3, 10

this. If you know that your friend Nancy really enjoys one particular restaurant in town, that she ohs and ahs at the mere suggestion of going there, no one would be surprised to find that you and your friends eat at Nancy's favorite place more than anyplace else. As a group you would probably be happier that way. Since no one has any reason to doubt the strength of Nancy's preferences and she continues to be ecstatic every time you go there, it's easy to give it special consideration. Friends automatically take strength of preference into account when they make decisions. It's only natural.

The difficulty comes when people who are not close friends must make a group decision. A competitive interaction, where their preferences are very dissimilar, can lead to mistrust and little motivation to reveal your true preferences.

One way that strength of preference enters these situations is vocally: The louder you shout, the stronger your preferences seem, and the more the group takes them into consideration. On the face of it, this suggestion sounds ludicrous. Just because someone can pierce another's eardrum doesn't necessarily mean that they have the strongest preferences.

But many groups implicitly translate loudness into strength of preference. As the old cliché goes, The squeaky wheel gets the grease. The most talkative group members usually get their way. Research also suggests that the alternative that is raised most frequently has the best chance of being chosen. Thus, shouting to convince other people that your preferences are stronger than theirs and simply repeating your preferred choice are tactics that are often successful. Unfortunately, if voice volume is not related to strength of preference, groups that are swayed by loud talkers are not making the best decisions.

Groups that are competitive and openly disagree often turn to voting to try to resolve their disputes. But voting is not the easy, reasonable procedure we often think it is. Take this situation: Three people are partners in a part-time enterprise that will soon sign a promotion contract with one of three performers. They don't have enough resources to sign all three, so they must limit their contract to one. Each of the partners wants control of the firm and each believes that signing their most preferred performer will give them an edge on the other two. If our three partners are Anne, Barbara, and Carol, and the three performers are X-Ray (X), Yellow Fever (Y), and Zorro's Children (Z), we might find that their preferences look like this:

	X-Ray	Yellow Fever	Zorro's Children
Anne	3	2	1
Barbara	2	1	3
Carol	1	3	2

Anne prefers X to Y, and Y to Z; Barbara prefers Z to X, and X to Y; and Carol prefers Y to Z, and Z to X. These are rankings, not strength of preference, since there's no good way for competitors to use strength of preference to make a fair group decision.

If they simply vote on their first preferences, no performer will be chosen; each will get a single vote. But they could use Robert's Rules of Order, a standard method for group decision making that parliamentary groups and congresses throughout the world use.

With Robert's Rules, they vote on two alternatives and

match the winner against the one remaining. Thus, if they consider X and Y first, Anne and Barbara would vote for X and Carol would vote for Y; X would win 2 to 1. Then, pairing X against Z leads to Anne voting for X and Barbara and Carol voting for Z. Thus, Z would win. It looks like Robert's Rules of Order will resolve the situation easily and fairly. They should sign Zorro's Children.

But the picture changes if they vote on X and Z first. Then Z would win the first vote (with Barbara and Carol's votes) and would be paired against Y. Anne and Carol would vote for Y, Barbara for Z, and Y would win. By changing the order of voting, we change the winner from Z to Y. Something is clearly wrong here.

And if they vote on Y and Z first, Y would win the first vote (with Anne and Carol's votes) but X would then beat Y with Anne and Barbara's votes. Now X is the overall winner.

In each case, the alternative that is voted on last is the one that wins. Clearly, this does not look like a good solution. Most people would agree that people's preferences, not the order of voting, should determine the final outcome.

Anne's, Barbara's, and Carol's preference are *cyclical:* As a group, they prefer X to Y and Y to Z. But they *also* prefer Z to X. Thus they prefer X to Y to Z to X to Y to Z to X . . . Around and around we go, with each alternative preferred to another. This may be why Nietzsche, the existential philosopher, said that madness was the exception in individuals but the rule in groups.

Groups' preferences are not necessarily transitive: If they prefer P to Q and Q to R, they may not prefer P to R. Individuals rarely have intransitive preferences, especially over simple issues. When someone prefers P to Q and Q to R, they generally prefer P to R. Thus, if you prefer coffee to tea and tea to milk, you generally prefer coffee to milk. Transitivity can go wrong, even for an individual, if the issue is complex enough. For instance, Bill may prefer a new car with a tape deck (B) to the new car without it (A). He may also prefer the new car with a tape deck and a sun roof (C) to the new car with a tape deck (B). Then he might prefer that the car also have a sports package (D) to the same car without the package. But when he compares the plain new car at its relatively low price (A) to the now extremely loaded car with its extremely loaded price (D), he may have a clear preference for simplicity (A). His preferences are intransitive: While he preferred D to C, C to B, and B to A, he also prefers A to D. A car dealer—who will rarely ask Bill to reconsider the stripped-down version of the car (A)—may be able to take advantage of this kind of intransitivity. But this situation is complicated and not very typical. Most often people have transitive preferences.

As the number of alternatives and the number of voters increase, intransitivities become much more likely in groups. A fair, representative group decision can become very elusive. Unfortunately, there is no clear solution for preference cycles: They are nuts that are almost impossible to crack fairly.

CONCLUSIONS

When a game is totally cooperative, like the Telephone Game, and it is in everyone's best interest to coordinate, the only problems come from miscommunication or other accidents. When different preferences come into play, however, a game can take a drastic shift. Then, a game's competitive elements can surface.

But even when preferences don't coincide, as in the Battle of the Sexes, both players may still prefer to do things together rather than apart. Chances for cooperation still remain. A mediator, an arbitrator, or an intravenor can help. Persuasion probably won't. If the disputants are good friends, they may investigate whether the strength of their preferences can help resolve their difficulties. If they aren't such great friends, they probably wouldn't mind going to separate events and wouldn't be playing the Battle of the Sexes.

The ending of these stories, then, concerns friendships: With it, bargaining is much easier. Without it, we lose one handy mechanism (strength of preference) for resolving disputes. This solution, true friendship, depends on the important concept of trust.

There are limits to how helpful trust can be, however. My mother has told me that she and Dad have long had an informal agreement, passed on from Grandma Murnighan. They love each other dearly, but they have an additional vow: "For better or for worse, but not for lunch." Maybe you shouldn't depend on friendship for too much.

CHAPTER 9

IRRATIONAL DECISIONS, OR GETTING CARRIED AWAY

People at an auction are bidding for a $20 bill. The rules require that the bids increase by a dollar each time. They started at $1 and went rapidly through $2, $3, $4, et cetera. At $15, things slowed down a bit, and only two people are now bidding. They go to $16, $17, $18 . . . $19 . . . $20, long pause . . . $21, $22, $23. What is going on here? Why would anyone ever pay more than $20 for a $20 bill?

The bids keep going, past $30, $40, $50, $60, $70; the same two people are doing all the bidding, back and forth. All for a $20 bill! This is not a group of lunatics. (It's also not for charity.) Instead, it's a group of executives at a bargaining seminar—and this is not such an unusual group; most groups end up bidding much more than $20 for a $20 bill. Groups regularly bid over $50, and sometimes over $100.

In the Dollar Auction, the highest bidder pays whatever he or she bid and receives the $20, just like at any other auction. The trick is that the second highest bidder also pays whatever he or she bid, but doesn't get anything. Thus, *the top two bidders both pay* what they bid, but only the highest of the two bidders gets the prize.

BIDDING IT UP

Like most auctions, the Dollar Auction generates a lot of interest for both bidders and nonbidders. In the old days, when a dollar was worth something, I ran the auction for a dollar, with no restrictions on the bids except that they exceed the previous bid. The bidding could start slowly, with early bids of a nickel, a dime, a quarter, before someone gets the idea of bidding 99 cents. Sometimes it went much faster, with someone bidding 99 cents right away.

For some reason the 99-cent bidders are almost always male. After their bids, they sit there with big, self-satisfied grins on their faces; they are clearly very proud of their little coups. For a minute, everyone else gives them a chance to bask in the glory of their creative ploy.

Invariably, however, someone bids $1, making the 99-cent bidder's smile instantly disappear. The new bidder has punctured the proud, 99-cent bidder's bubble and simultaneously presented him with a dilemma: He'll lose 99 cents if he lets things stand, but he'll have to bid more than $1 to win the $1 prize. While he's thinking about his choices, the new bidder is enjoying the fact that he has wiped a big smile off his competitor's face and everyone else buzzes with excitement. They can't help but appreciate the new bidder's ego-deflating maneuver.

The original 99-cent bidder invariably bids $1.01. Everyone breaks up laughing at the thought that someone has just bid more than $1 to get $1. Then the auction settles down to a test of wills between the last two bidders, who must negotiate how much they will lose.

They face three issues: (1) How much can I afford to lose? (2) How can I look tough enough to scare the other bidder out of bidding more? And (3) how do I get out of this predicament without looking like a total fool? One person trying to look tough often leads to the other bidder trying the same strategy. Then both reap greater and greater losses (financial and reputational) than they would if they had just stopped bidding. The only winner is the auctioneer—me. (My favorite charities win, too.)

The bidders tend to be much more concerned with pride than money. In a group of executives several years ago, the two last bidders were the president of a real estate firm and a local judge in the federal court system. The real estate man had just completed a wonderfully profitable year; the judge collected old Mercedes-Benz automobiles. Clearly, the costs of this game (I was only auctioning $1) were insignificant to both of them.

Their bidding proceeded quite rapidly, with each trying to convince the other that he wouldn't back down. It was clear that neither of them wanted to be shown up in the bidding.

At one point one of them bid $3.00. The other's next bid was $4.25. I couldn't help pausing at this point, even though that is not what a good auctioneer should do. If both bidders were strictly rational, the $4.25 bid should have ended the auction. It exceeded the previous bid by more than $1.00; thus, the other bidder would only lose *more* by bidding any further. Instead, the $3.00 bidder almost immediately bid $4.50. Needless to say, that brought a roar from the group. In fact, the $4.25 bidder reported later that his bid was not meant to be a rational, let's-stop-the-auction-here-and-I'll-lose-more-than-you-do bid. Instead, it was just another attempt to look tough by raising the bid that much more.

In large groups (twenty or more), I always auction off several dollars, one right after the other. People have a very hard time trying to band together and collude. A group of thirty-three people, for instance, would realize a profit of only 3 cents each if they stopped the bidding at a penny and shared equally in the winnings. Someone is always tempted to bid slightly higher, and once one person bids 5 or 10 cents, everyone else is reluctant to let the defector win. Thus, someone else will also bid, especially when the auctioneer controls the bidding.

All it takes to win money is to have two people bid 50 cents or more. Bidders usually don't realize that—they're too emotionally involved. Even the nonbidders tend to focus their attention on bids that exceed $1. Seeing someone bid more than $1 to win $1 is a perverse pleasure for almost everyone. But from the auctioneer's perspective, once two people bid more than 50 cents, the rest is all profit.

STRATEGIES

After the first auction, everyone sees that the second highest bidder always has an incentive to bid more than the highest bidder; the potential gain of the $1 bill offsets the cost of increasing their bid. Add a little pride and it's clear that backing out can be very difficult. Thus, many people realize that the game itself establishes forces that encourage the last two bidders to continue bidding. The optimal strategy in this game is not to bid at all—unless you are the only bidder, or no one is willing to go beyond low bids (a truly uncertain prospect).

Second and third runs of the auction continue to generate profits (for me). People who lose money in the earlier auctions often bid again in hopes of winning back some of their losses. As we have seen with other games, one reason for this ineffective strategy is emotional: People who get involved in the bidding are more emotionally caught up in the task and have a harder time seeing its ramifications. People who haven't bid in the first auction usually don't bid in subsequent auctions. Not getting involved the first time gives them an edge in subsequent plays. They affirm one of Abraham Lincoln's famous quotes: "It is better to keep your mouth shut and be thought a fool than to open it and remove all doubt."

ESCALATING COMMITMENT

People often get into things and suddenly find that they're in over their heads. The Dollar Auction is about overinvolvement, how just getting started can sometimes lead to getting more and more and more involved. The United States defense system provides many examples of this phenomenon: New weapons are sometimes outdated by production time. Private-sector organizations suffer from the same problem. Many computer firms, for instance, have found that they get enmeshed in deciding whether to invest in a new product and, by the time it has been designed and produced, another firm has beaten them to the market with a product that's more advanced than theirs. This phenomenon also afflicts individuals. One scenario that might be familiar to many people is the overinvolvement that sometimes follows an initial step toward romance. Andrea's story provides a simple example.

Andrea is a young vice-president at one of the major banks in town. She's not married and is not seeing anyone regularly. She is at a cocktail party and finds that her eye is caught, almost involuntarily, by a man across the room. It also appears that she has caught his eye. Eventually they strike up a conversation; they seem to find each other attractive and interesting. He's not seeing anyone either, so when Andrea asks herself whether she should see him again, her answer is an easy one: "Why not?" So they go out for a drink. Then they go out for dinner and then a movie and all of a sudden they are seeing each other on a regular basis. While that is happening, a voice inside Andrea's head occasionally tells her that even though she's having a good time, she's not having a really great time. (He may be hearing the same kind of voice.) It's not a loud voice, so she doesn't pay much attention to it. Before you know it, though, Andrea is romantically involved; she's even beginning to feel the tug of a commitment. She discovers that it's easier to see him than to try to meet someone new. With no trouble at all, and no conscious decision on her part, Andrea has found herself involved in a romance—but not an overwhelmingly exciting romance. She gradually gets more and more involved and it becomes harder and harder to extract herself from this relationship. She meets some of his friends; he meets some of hers; everybody soon expects to see them together at social events. If either of them is alone, friends ask where the other is.

As all this develops, Andrea's Romantic Pain Potential (RPP) increases; at the same time, her Romantic Gain Potential (RGP) drops. Before too long, RPP dominates RGP. A difficult ending becomes the next logical step. Andrea's story is not happy, but it has repeated itself often, for many, many people. And some of the dynamics of her romantic experience (not all of them) are nicely captured in the Dollar Auction.

Not surprisingly, research has shown that people who set limits for themselves before beginning the Dollar Auction do better. They are not always successful at being restrained by their stated limit, but they tend to bid less than people who don't set limits. The problem with romances and other adventures is that it's hard to pause and set limits ahead of time. Instead, we hope for everything and pay less attention to the downside.

Too Much Invested to Quit

Barry Staw, a professor at the University of California at Berkeley, and his colleagues have conducted several research projects to investigate how commitment to a failed course of action can escalate. Business students read the fictitious case of the Adams and Smith Company, which has had a long, profitable history but now looks like it's in trouble. Acting as financial vice-presidents, students are asked to invest $10 million in either the company's Consumer or Industrial products division.

After they have made their decision, time is accelerated to five years later. Half of the VPs are told that their original decisions were successful: The division that received the extra funds had turned itself around and looked as if it would continue to be successful for some time. The other VPs are told that their decisions were not successful: The division that had received the influx of money was doing worse than ever. After this news, they must invest up to $20 million more in either of the two divisions, Consumer or Industrial products; this time they can divide the money any way they like.

People whose previous decisions were *unsuccessful* pour *more* money into that same, failing division. Not only that, when they also face a serious personal threat (that is, losing their job as financial VP), they commit *even more* to the unsuccessful division. Commitments do not escalate, however, when decision makers know that they will be throwing good money after bad. Only when they have hope of escaping the costs of previous poor decisions do decision makers escalate their commitments.

People escalate and commit themselves to a course of action when (1) they think that future gains are possible, (2) they are optimistic that they can turn a project around, (3) they're publicly committed or identified with the project, or (4) they can get much of their investment back if the project fails.

Most of these forces come into play in the Dollar Auction Game. Bidders drop out if they don't mind taking a loss or if they are less ego-involved in the bidding and don't feel that they have to win at all costs. They continue when they think they can still gain by bidding, and when they think they can still be a winner.

Escalating commitment is insidious—it creeps up on you and, before you know it, you're much more committed than you want to be. Stories of how innocent people have gotten involved in the Mafia are an example drawn from the popular media. The history of the Vietnam War is another example: Once the first serviceman was killed overseas, America's involvement in the war escalated. With each successive casualty, involvement increased more, even though early intelligence reports indicated that waging a successful war in Southeast Asia was highly unlikely.

Investment fiascoes provide numerous examples. People often buy a stock when they think it's a good deal and, when it goes down, *they often buy more of the same stock,* since now it's an even better deal. Commitment and investment can easily escalate, and mean serious financial losses.

There are times when you get involved in something and, all of a sudden, you find that you have become overinvolved. It's a kind of commitment that seems to have a life all its own; you don't really feel like you're in control of the situation at all. Examples abound. A friend once told me this true story: A couple he knows moved to a new town and joined the synagogue in their neighborhood. The couple felt like they had paid quite a lot to join. They began going regularly to the synagogue's social get-togethers and, after attending several, complained that they were having a terrible time, week after week. When asked why they didn't stop going, they replied, "Well, we paid all this money to join. We don't want it to go to waste."

SUNK COSTS

The Dollar Auction is unlike typical auctions. If we simply auctioned off a dollar bill, the bids would certainly go to 99 cents. Someone might even bid a dollar if they got some value from winning. But the introduction of a second bidder who must also pay contributes to a tremendous increase in the bids.

The key elements that lead to escalating commitment are (1) free choice at the very beginning and (2) negative consequences, which (3) you think you have the opportunity to overcome. It's hard to stop a commitment that's escalating.

Several years ago I owned a sporty, imported car. It was a wonderful car to drive. Unfortunately, it was not a wonderful car to fix. When it had accumulated a few miles, it needed more and more repairs. The difficulty was that my commitment to the car escalated every time I paid a new repair bill. I freely chose to buy the car and to have it fixed when it broke down. Thus, I fulfilled step number one in escalating commitment. When things broke, I paid quite a bit to get the car in working order again. I implicitly thought of each of these repair bills as investments ("Now that I've fixed this, it's bound to run well."). The more I spent, the more committed I became. Negative consequences, element number 2, were more and more fulfilled the more I paid for repairs. The escalation continued, of course, because the longer I kept the car, the more it broke down, the more I paid for repairs, and the more committed I became.

Finally, I hit my mileage limit for a car—after a car hits 80,000 miles, I feel like I should sell it. I have a hard time trusting the car to work on long trips when it has so many miles, so I invoke my informal rule that this is the time to sell. Thank goodness for the rule—without it, I may have gotten even more committed to that car. In the end, I developed a real love-hate relationship with it, possibly like Andrea and her romance or investors and their failing stocks.

The moral of this story is to beware of escalating commitment. It's a disease that can creep up and grab you and not let go. The crux of the problem is the commitment's *sunk costs:*

Once we've invested, whether it's time, effort, or money, we value the investment and have a tremendously hard time abandoning it. It may be water over the dam or spilled milk, but if we feel that the water or the milk cost us a lot, we have a hard time ignoring it. We don't think of sunk costs as sunk. So we're susceptible to pouring good money (or effort or time) after bad, It's very hard to avoid.

One last anecdote about the Dollar Auction. I described the Dollar Auction to a German friend who is a dealer in antique books and prints. He attends art auctions all the time. In fact, that is a major part of his work; he buys and sells at auctions around the world. He said that the rules of the Dollar Auction are often used by German charities. That way they raise more money. He also said that they call it "An American Auction."

CHAPTER 10

THE
VOLUNTEER
DILEMMA

A group of penguins is standing on an ice floe. It's cold near the South Pole, but that doesn't bother them. What *is* bothering them is hunger—they haven't eaten for some time and they're starting to get restless. Many of them move to the edge of the floe and peer into the water. They know there are fish down there, but they're afraid that there may also be a killer whale—or that a walrus may be hungry, too. So, they are *very* hesitant about plunging in. At least for the moment, they hover by the edge of the ice, looking and looking.

A somewhat different theatrical scene is happening at the same time in an open field in the United States. A group of small birds is feeding on the seeds that have fallen in a farmer's field. They are all quite happy at their find, and they're stocking up, eating hungrily. Each of them occasionally pauses to look up into the sky, checking to see whether a large predator may be flying overhead. If anyone spots such a beast, he must sound the alarm because they would be very easy prey sitting in the open. At another spot in the field, a short distance away, a group of ground squirrels is doing just what the birds are doing, eating away while keeping an eye open for big, hungry birds flying overhead. If such a threat appears, the group member who sees the danger has a difficult choice. Should she call out the alarm, allowing everyone a chance to get away, but at the same time drawing attention to herself? A hungry predator who sees their group will be attracted to it and will almost automatically steer toward the individual that sounds the alarm. But if no one warns the others, everyone is threatened with even greater danger. What will each of them do if a predator comes?

The penguins, the little birds, and the ground squirrels are all faced with a volunteer dilemma. Before we reveal how they have solved it, let's see how people react to the dilemma of volunteering.

Most of the volunteering situations we face don't force us to make life-and-death decisions like the penguins', small birds', and ground squirrels'. Wartime, however, can generate even more threatening dilemmas. U.S. Army manuals, for instance, indicate that if you are involved in trench warfare and a live grenade lands in your trench, you should cover it with your body and protect your colleagues from the effects of its explosion. If the grenade goes off, it means almost certain death. Similarly, many Japanese pilots volunteered to act as kamikazes, using their planes as bombs by flying directly into enemy ships.

Most volunteer dilemmas are less serious, but still involve the difficult choice between volunteering yourself and hoping that someone else will do the honors. Our research, understandably, has avoided life-and-death decisions. Instead, we have focused on the possibility of gaining rather than of losing. Here is an example:

You are in a room with ninety-nine strangers. It might be a reception area or a waiting room at an airport. A distinguished-looking individual with sparkling eyes comes up to all of you and says, "I have a proposition for you. I would be willing to pay many of you one hundred thousand dollars if at least one of you is willing to accept one thousand dollars. You may not talk about it or communicate with each other in any way. You must simply think about what you want to choose, and write down either one thousand dollars or one hundred thousand dollars on a small slip of paper. If at least one of you chooses one thousand dollars, all of you will get what you asked for. If everyone asks for one hundred thousand dollars, however, none of you will get anything. You have one minute to make up your mind." Your benefactor then has you and the strangers sit so you can't really see each other and waits for your response.

If you were in this situation, what would you write on your slip of paper: $1,000 or $100,000? Also, what would you do if twenty volunteers were required? Would that change your decision? What about forty, or sixty, or eighty?

VOLUNTEERING

We have studied situations where the group includes from two to one hundred people, where one to eighty volunteers are required, where volunteers get fictitious payoffs between $2 and $1,000, and nonvolunteers can get fictitious payoffs up to $100,000.

When a volunteer can get $1,000 and a nonvolunteer can get $2,000, there are almost always enough volunteers, regardless of the size of the group or the number of volunteers required (within the limits of our investigations). When one volunteer is needed from a group of ten people, we've found a large surplus of volunteers—almost 60 percent volunteered. That means that half of the group has settled for $1,000 less than they had to, which is not very efficient. Even when the scenario requires that eight out of ten people volunteer, there are still plenty of volunteers—94 percent, on average.

That doesn't happen, however, when nonvolunteers can get $10,000 or $100,000. Then some groups don't provide enough volunteers and everyone gets nothing. Thus, if our distinguished-looking individual with the sparkling eyes wanted to play the game and not lose any money, she might want to try a combination of $1,000 for the volunteers, $10,000 for the nonvolunteers, and require 80 percent of the group to volunteer. The desire to win $10,000 is strong enough to tempt enough people that, on average, only 76 percent volunteer. With the prize for nonvolunteers at $100,000, only 67 percent volunteer—$100,000 is very enticing.

Even when only one volunteer is needed from a group of

one hundred, volunteer(s) can receive $1,000, and nonvolunteers can receive $100,000, we get too many volunteers—13 percent on average. A really efficient group would have only one. If everyone could talk to one another, they could reach such an agreement. The ability to communicate would make the task both very easy and very lucrative; it would be agreed, for example, that the volunteer would receive a $1,000 kickback from everyone in the group—and even if some members reneged, he would still make out very well.

Certainly everyone is tempted by a $100,000 payoff. Indeed, this situation is a dream come true for most people. The question then becomes: Why does anyone settle for $1,000? Volunteers say that (1) they wanted to assure themselves of $1,000, which for them is a lot of money; (2) they wanted to make sure that everyone who asked for it got $100,000; or (3) they expected to get some additional money from the big winners.

The first group is straightforward: They chose $1,000 because they don't want to lose this opportunity completely. They're being risk averse and the smaller payoff is valuable to them. The second group identify themselves as true altruists, doing for others even though they themselves benefit much less. Research has frequently shown, however, that true altruists constitute a very small percentage of the population (5 percent or less). Thus, we might question the second group's sincerity—people are usually more likely to say they are altruistic than they are to act altruistically.

People who expect others to give them part of their $100,000 are the most interesting. They have concocted an elaborate story even though (1) there is no way for them to arrange any redistribution of the money ahead of time; (2) they are interacting with total strangers; and (3) they have no idea how the money will actually be paid. They have an imagination, and they have faith. In truth, they may not be able to contact the winners after the money is distributed; and they don't know how those people will react even if they do reach them. Will the big winner believe that they volunteered? And if they do, will they give some of their winnings away? Unfortunately, there is *no* information in the scenario to verify their picture of the situation. But it does justify their choice to volunteer.

We also ask people who volunteered, after everything is all over, to make the following choice: Which would make you more unhappy: (1) if you were the only person to volunteer or (2) if there were thirty volunteers out of one hundred in the group? A startling majority say that they would be more unhappy if they were the only volunteer.

Many people want to be reassured that there are other kind people, like themselves, in the world. That is a lot like the misery-loves-company idea, which research results have refined to mean "misery loves *miserable* company." Being the only volunteer makes people upset at the thought that so many people are not like themselves, but are greedy.

Would a seasoned negotiator react in this way? If someone else is volunteering, it makes no sense to volunteer: It is inefficient from a group standpoint, since volunteering doesn't help anyone; and from an individual standpoint, you needlessly lose $99,000. The big bonanza is only a whisper away and, by unnecessarily volunteering, you lose a small fortune.

But if you are the only volunteer among one hundred people, you actually increase your outcome by $1,000. If you hadn't volunteered, no one would have gotten anything, including you. Our distinguished-looking individual with the sparkling eyes would go away with all the money and an ironic grin. So being the only volunteer is important—important to you to the tune of $1,000 and important to everyone else to the tune of $100,000. In addition, your single voluntary choice means that the entire group is perfectly efficient. A seasoned negotiator should not be unhappy with this. But most people are not so philosophical. It makes them unhappy to think that they are the only one to volunteer, and it also makes them angry at the people they've helped so much—even when their speculations about people's reasons for choosing $100,000 are unverifiable. Clearly, their reaction is personal and emotional, not coolly rational. We are social animals and we rarely want to act as solitary altruists. If we were identified by everyone as the hero of the situation, or our picture were on the front page of national newspapers, or the President gave us a medal in a fancy public ceremony, maybe then our solitary act of volunteering would make us happy. We could publish a book about our experiences and sell the screen rights. But, again, just as with the stories people formulated when they expected other members of the group to reward them when they volunteered, there is not much basis for these fantasies either.

What about nonvolunteers? In our experiments, we ask people to respond to several of these scenarios, with various prizes, group sizes, and so on. Some (about 10 percent) *always* choose not to volunteer, regardless of the potential payoffs. Some figure that when there is little difference between the high and low prize, many people will settle for the smaller prize, increasing everyone else's chances for the larger payoff. Thus, when the choice is between $1,000 for volunteers and $2,000 for nonvolunteers, they assume that there will be several volunteers, so they might as well go for the $2,000. When the prizes get larger (for example, $10,000 or $100,000), the high prize becomes too tempting, and they feel compelled to choose it. This group of people might be labeled the Small Prize Rational, High Prize Emotional group. Their thinking isn't consistent, but who ever said people have to be consistent?

The other explanation for choosing the high number all the time is the expectation that *someone* is always bound to volunteer. This "Always Optimistic" group figures that people can volunteer for many different reasons and that even in a group where you don't know anyone, some of those reasons are bound to take effect. If they don't—if no one is an altruist, if no one is happy with the unexpected bonus of the smaller payoff, if no one feels that people expect them to volunteer—then you just chalk it up to experience and you're no worse off than you were when you began. In fact, you have a new variation on an old story—The Big One That Got Away.

MULTIPLE VOLUNTEERS

When more than one volunteer is needed, pessimism increases as the number of volunteers required increases. When more than half the group must volunteer, many people despair at their chances of winning. That leads some people to choose the high payoff fatalistically, thinking they have no chance at it, rather than choosing to volunteer and increasing their chances for some prize.

In this way, people contribute to a *self-fulfilling prophecy:* By predicting that not enough people will volunteer, and basing their own actions on their prediction, they increase the chances that their prediction will be fulfilled—that enough people *won't* volunteer, and that they won't win anything. This is much like the maître d' who thinks that young people don't give good tips and therefore seats them at the worst table in a restaurant. By doing so, he increases the chances that they will not leave a good tip.

This self-fulfilling prophecy is most often true when 80 percent of the group must volunteer to win. When few volunteers are needed (20 percent or less), a surplus of volunteers is normal. For instance, when the group is twenty-five people, needing one volunteer leads to 23 percent volunteering; needing two leads to 30 percent. People don't accelerate their volunteering as much as they should when the required number of volunteers increases, but for small numbers of required volunteers, it's still enough.

WORK

Many times people are asked to volunteer to do some extra work. They may get paid for it, formally or informally, but it still means extra work. More often, the extra work gets them no extra pay. Take the following example.

You work for a company that hires people to work independently. You are one of one hundred people, all strangers, who work alone in their homes. Your boss calls you with an unusual but intriguing proposition. She says that she needs some extra work done. She's looking for some of you to work on an additional task that will take sixty hours. As compensation, she would pay some of you $10,000 *if* at least twenty of you were willing to do the work for $1,000. You may not talk about it or communicate with any of the others since you don't know who they are. You must simply think about whether you would be willing to do the work, and if you were, whether you would want to be paid $1,000 or $10,000. If at least twenty of you do the work for $1,000, then they will be paid $1,000, and everyone else who works will be paid the $10,000 they asked for. If fewer than twenty choose to work for $1,000, everyone will be notified before the work is to begin, and no one will do any extra work or get any extra pay. At least twenty people must be willing to work for $1,000 for everyone to get paid what they asked for. Would you do the extra work, and if so, would you ask for $1,000 or $10,000?

By adding work to the volunteer dilemma, a peculiar thing happens: People become less willing to volunteer. Theoretically, that shouldn't happen. Volunteers and nonvolunteers work the same amount; they just get different payoffs, exactly as the earlier, nonwork volunteers did in our previous scenario.

The addition of work seems to add the issue of merit. Without having to work, everyone can think of the prize as a bonus. With work entering the equation, however, volunteers feel even more negatively toward nonvolunteers. The notion of equal work for equal pay is powerful; it can really make the number of volunteers dwindle.

ANIMAL STRATEGIES

Let's return to our friends the animals. The ground squirrels, the little birds, and the penguins all react differently to their life and death dilemmas. The ground squirrels may fear that sounding a warning will increase their chances of being the predator's target. It's difficult to volunteer unless you know that you, your family, and friends are close to your hole and your chance for escape. I can't help envisioning a ground squirrel seeing a hawk and tiptoeing toward his hole prior to sounding the alarm. I don't know that this happens, but research does indicate that calling out the alarm happens faster when a ground squirrel is near family members. The evolutionary explanation (save your genes) seems to apply here.

The birds have discovered an optimal solution to help protect themselves and their volunteers. When one bird squawks to sound the alarm, they all take off in a flock, and allow the volunteer to fly in the middle. Whoever volunteers knows that she will be the least threatened and that it pays to volunteer. That is an ingenious solution to their dilemma.

The penguins are also crafty, but their solution is not so neat. As they all move to the edge of their ice floe, hoping that someone else will volunteer, they jostle around and *push* one penguin into the water. The term *volunteer* works here as a passive verb: One of the penguins *is volunteered.* (Hasn't everyone experienced being volunteered? For, one hopes, a less dangerous task?) As a result, the penguins sometimes lose one of their group and must wait hungrily until it's time to volunteer someone else. Needless to say, that is a pretty morbid solution to the volunteer dilemma.

As groups get larger, the chances of someone volunteering goes up. It's easier to get one volunteer from a group of one hundred than from a group of ten. The need for any single individual to be the volunteer, however, goes down. People often volunteer when they feel that they are critical for the entire group, but when the need for them to play a critical role goes down (that is, in large groups), so does the frequency of volunteers. Thus, while ten people may volunteer in a group of one hundred, a larger proportion (more than one in ten) is likely in a smaller group.

ALTRUISM

The tendency for fewer people to volunteer in large groups has been used to explain one of the most bizarre incidents ever reported in the American press. Some years ago, a young woman named Kitty Genovese was murdered in New York City. Although murder is not uncommon in big cities, the details surrounding this murder were very unusual. They were revealed two weeks later in a front-page story.

The murderer took thirty-five minutes, in three separate attacks, to kill his victim. He was scared away during his first two attacks due to people turning on lights in their apartment windows in the area. But he persisted, and returned, and stabbed her during each of three attacks until she finally died. Investigation revealed that thirty-eight people witnessed the crime and only a single witness called the police—after the third attack and after Kitty Genovese was dead.

Analyses following this event decried the apathy that can infect people who live in big cities. But further, more systematic investigations suggested that the presence of so many witnesses may have led each of them to believe that *someone else* was reporting the crime. No one felt critical; everyone thought that someone else was calling or had called the police.

The same kind of phenomenon can work in the volunteer dilemma. If you are the only one who can turn the tide and you know you're critical, the odds are quite good that you will volunteer, especially if (1) you're a seasoned negotiator, (2) there's no danger involved, or (3) your payoff is reasonably high. If lots of other people can volunteer and you can benefit from not volunteering, your motivation to volunteer will probably drop. No one volunteered to call the police to help save Kitty Genovese until it was too late—possibly because there were so many witnesses. If only one apartment light had been turned on and the sole witness could see that he was the only one who could report the crime, he might have been more likely to call. Kitty Genovese may have died because so many people responded to her screams by turning on their lights. Unfortunately, the witnesses also responded to each other rather than notifying the police themselves.

CERTAINTY AND UNCERTAINTY

Strategically, then, everyone considers the benefits for volunteering, the benefits for not volunteering, and the probability that someone else will volunteer, especially when only a single volunteer is needed. Paradoxically, being certain that someone will volunteer may lead everyone not to volunteer. If you know the other group members well and trust each other implicitly, you may expect that someone will do the "right" thing. Being certain *and* correct is obviously helpful; being certain and incorrect can spell disaster.

Uncertainty, then, should increase the likelihood that someone will volunteer. Being certain that no one will volunteer may be better than being certain that someone will volunteer, because a seasoned negotiator who can reap real gains from volunteering may decide to volunteer. Thus, a more cooperative, effective solution may arise when people are uncertain about each others' actions.

CONCLUSIONS

The concept of volunteering is critical in both the public and private sectors. It is also critical in less formal environments, including groups of family and friends. Most organized entities would simply not function if no one volunteered. For example, worker slowdowns often take the form of *adhering* to the company's formal rules—strictly. By sticking to the letter of the law, workers can hamstring an organization and slow its productivity tremendously. Only when informal, voluntary inputs are provided can groups and organizations—families, small companies, service centers—function efficiently and effectively.

Examples are abundant and far outweigh and outnumber the activities we usually label as voluntary. In addition to hospital work, raising funds for charities, and contributing brownies for the community rummage sale, other cases of volunteering include (1) someone staying late at work to make absolutely certain that a report is finished and finished well for tomorrow morning's presentation; (2) someone doing the dishes after dinner because the family member who regularly washes them had a particularly trying day; (3) one member of a couple nursing the other back to health when the flu strikes; (4) the boss making coffee for the secretary, rather than vice versa; (5) someone in the firm offering to show a foreign visitor how things work in the company and taking valuable time away from her desk to do so; and (6) an old employee retiring and a colleague giving a short speech at the retirement party.

The list can go on and on. One aspect of all these examples that comes shining through is that the act of volunteering helps to solidify the group and the volunteer's place within the group. Families are tighter when they all work for each other; bosses and their secretaries respect each other more; and couples have an easier time ironing out their problems when they volunteer for each other whenever the need arises.

The act of volunteering, and overcoming the volunteer dilemma, strengthens group ties and lays the groundwork for the members to overcome other dilemmas. Thus we can make perfect sense of the choice to volunteer for $1,000 instead of $10,000 when only one person out of a hundred is necessary. Thinking that other members of the group will contribute some of their winnings to you because you volunteered is a way of justifying your original volunteering behavior. Some people volunteer because they have strong expectations that that act and other we-are-a-group acts go together. When group bonds are very strong, they lay the groundwork for *pervasive cooperation,* where everyone benefits. The act of volunteering, itself a dilemma, is one way of pushing closer to systemic, taken-for-granted cooperation.

CHAPTER 11

THE WINNER'S CURSE

Anatol Rapoport, a truly eminent scholar and energetic seeker of peace, recently told a delightful story about a game he and his older brother played when they were children. He called it the Highest Number Game. To play the game, each of them thought of a number; whoever came up with the highest number won the game. Clearly, it's not very difficult, and is just the kind of game that two precocious kids might play.

Dr. Rapoport's brother was the first to learn of the concept of infinity. As a result, he was excited to play the Highest Number Game and was even willing to go first. He immediately came out with "Infinity!" Young Anatol pondered for a bit, as he didn't know what infinity was, but he figured it must be a pretty big number. He finally discovered what he thought was a winner: "Infinity plus one!"

The Rapoport brothers soon tired of the Highest Number Game, but it still holds some intrigue. Douglas Hofstadter, in his "Metamagical Themas" column in *Scientific American,* related it to his (fictitious) Platonia Dilemma. The Platonia Dilemma goes like this: You receive a letter from a Mr. Platonia, whom you know to be incredibly wealthy. It says that you and nineteen other leading rational thinkers have received the letter. Each of you has a chance to win one billion dollars. If within forty-eight hours, one and only one of you sends a telegram with your name on it to the Platonia Institute, you will receive the billion. If more than one person sends in his name, no one wins. The offer will be rescinded if any of you tries to contact any of the others. In addition, the winner will have to agree not to share the prize with any of the others in the group. Thus, cooperation is ruled out.

The question is, what would everyone do? What would you do? Since Hofstadter couldn't ask anyone to really respond to the Platonia Dilemma, he investigated a different, less lucrative dilemma—the prisoner's dilemma, which we considered in Chapter 4 in our discussion of the Gas Station Game. He reasoned that the actions of twenty people who were very familiar with the game would give us some idea of how people might respond to the Platonia Dilemma. So he sent the following set of payoffs to twenty selected people, mostly social scientists, and asked them to make a single choice: A or B.

| | | Party 2 | |
		A	B
Party 1	A	$3, $3	0, $5
	B	$5, 0	$1, $1

Each of the twenty was required to respond within twenty-hours of the time that he received Hofstadter's letter. If all twenty cooperated (that is, chose A), each would win $57—$3 for each of the other nineteen cooperators. If they all defected (chose B), each would receive $19. If one person defected and nineteen cooperated, the defector would receive $5 for each cooperator, or a total of $95. The cooperators would receive $54 each (nothing for the defector and $3 for the other eighteen).

Many in Hofstadter's group had a difficult time deciding. They talked about how logic led them in circles as they tried to decide. Some said that because it was a one-shot game, there was no reason to do anything other than defect. Others said they defected because their payoff was always larger by defecting. One person flipped a coin. Some felt better cooperating and did so. One did not want it to be known in a widely circulating magazine that he had defected; he cooperated too.

Trying to make this choice can put you in a vicious circle. Think of it this way: If everyone cooperates, the group maximizes its gain. Thus, it pays for everyone to cooperate. But if everyone cooperates, why not be the sole defector and get $95, the maximum payoff? By doing that, you don't reduce anyone else's payoffs by very much. But if everyone thinks that way, everyone will defect. And around it goes. Hofstadter's final results? Fourteen defections; six cooperators.

And what about the Platonia Dilemma? How would you solve that? Hofstadter suggests a solution where all twenty people find a twenty-sided die and make their choice on the basis of the roll of the die. If you roll the number 1, submit your name; otherwise don't. This maximizes the chances that you would be the winner if you rolled a 1—*if* everyone stuck to their guns and didn't submit their name anyway, when their roll wasn't 1. If there is only one roll of a 1 (which is likely but not certain), someone will win. Everyone has a one-in-twenty chance to win $1 billion, or expected values of $50 million each. Not a bad deal. If you were actually playing this game and discovered this solution, what would you do if you didn't roll a 1? Wouldn't you be tempted to try another roll? In the end, it probably wouldn't surprise too many of us to hear that more than one name was sent in.

THE NEW HIGHEST NUMBER GAME

Let's return now to high numbers. I often give groups the chance to play the New Highest Number Game for a prize of $100. Everyone writes down a number. The person with the highest number wins $100 *divided* by the total of everyone's numbers. A high number increases your chances of winning, but a low number, if it wins, maximizes your prize. The higher the number you submit, the lower the prize if you win.

If you submit a low number, you must depend on everyone else to submit even smaller numbers. The key here is to submit a number that is just larger than everyone else's. That requires a lot of information about the others' numbers. Since you would rarely have such information, your dilemma remains. If you were playing, what would your number be?

If everyone colludes, one person can bid 1 (or less), everyone else can bid 0, and the group will take me for the whole $100. Someone designated by all will win the prize and can distribute it as they had decided.

In a recent group of experienced bargainers, many people chose 1 or less. Most of the rest of the choices were between 1 and 10. There was a single 10; the winner submitted 11. He correctly figured that someone would bid 10, and that he would have to bid just a little more. The group's numbers totaled fifty, so the winner got $2—not a big take. But it was considerably better than many inexperienced groups do; then, someone always chooses numbers exceeding 100—usually much, much more. These high numbers win, but the prize is almost always less than a penny. This may be a case where the drive to win actually gets in the way of optimal performance. It's a lot like focusing on a good score when you're playing golf; by concentrating on the final outcome, you forget about the process that's needed to get there. Thus, golfers who are having a good round and begin to focus on their score can easily forget about concentrating on the next shot. If they hit it poorly, they may press that much harder on the next shot and forget that they need to hit a single well-executed shot before they can hope for a good score. Focusing on winning may mean that you lose along the way.

THE LURING LOTTERY

The New Highest Number Game is more than a child's game, especially when there's a big prize. Indeed, Hofstadter emulated his Platonia Dilemma with a version of the New Highest Number Game. *Scientific American* sponsored the contest and put up a prize of $1 million—yes, $1 million.

The "Luring Lottery" allowed anyone and everyone to submit whatever number they wished. The prize was $1 million divided by the total of all the entries. Thus, if only one person submitted a 1, she would win the $1 million. But the prize would drop quickly with each new submission, especially high numbers.

The circulation of the English version of *Scientific American* was approximately 660,000 at the time. If 10,000 people read the article and thought about responding, how many entries would you expect? Readers knew the results of Hofstadter's twenty-person prisoner's dilemma game and his solution to the Platonia Dilemma. To implement his solution here, they should have found a die with many sides (less than ten thousand) and submitted an entry only if their roll of the die was a 1. That way there would have been very few entries and someone would win a lot of money.

Instead, there were about 2,000 entries. Over half (1,133) submitted the number 1. Other prominent numbers were also popular:

Number Entered	Number of Entries
1	1,139
10	49
100	61
1000	46
1 million	33
1 billion	11

Each of the entries of 1 billion cut the prize, all by itself, to one tenth of a cent. But these weren't the largest entries. Nine people submitted *a googol*, which is 10^{100}; fourteen submitted *a googolplex*, which is 10^{googol}. These are some big numbers. Several other entrants strained to come up with even higher numbers. Some filled their postcard with 9s; others submitted complicated mathematical formulas. As Hofstadter notes: "It is not clear that I, or for that matter anyone else, would be able to determine which is the largest integer submitted."

AUCTIONS

The Highest Number Game and the Luring Lottery have all the characteristics of an auction. Auctions happen everywhere, in country towns, where farms and their contents are put up for bid; in cities, where artwork, jewels, or real estate is auctioned; and in the boardrooms of government, where firms bid on defense contracts. Auctions have a variety of different rules that can be very important strategically (as we saw in the Dollar Auction Game).

In the most common form, the English auction, the highest bidder receives the prize and pays what he bid for it—if the bid exceeds the seller's reservation price, the lowest price she will accept. If it doesn't, what looks like a sale actually isn't. This frequently happens in art auctions, and occasionally in wine auctions.

In a Dutch auction, so named because it is how tulips were sold in Holland, a high price for the object is posted and is gradually lowered until someone can wait no longer and accepts it, before it tempts someone else. Thus, everyone waits nervously until he sees a price he likes—if he's lucky. If he waits too long, someone else will obtain the object, albeit for a higher price. By waiting, you risk losing the object while hoping to get it for a reduced price. The trade-off can be nerve-racking.

Auctions are particularly interesting because people put different values on the objects being auctioned. An old impressionist painting, for instance, can fetch a wide range of bids for two reasons. First, people really don't know how much it's worth. Its *objective* value is not clear. At the same time, people have different feelings about the painting; its *subjective* value also varies. Collectors, for instance, may value an object more than other people do. Auctioneers count on this I have-to-have-it emotion to boost the bids.

Alan Bond, an Australian tycoon, recently paid over $50 million at auction for "The Irises" by Vincent Van Gogh. Most professional buyers said at the time of his purchase that he had paid too much, but their pronouncements sounded like sour grapes. When Bond's financial empire went into rapid decline, however, he was forced to sell the painting for an undisclosed but apparently much lower price, and those early observations gained considerable credibility.

When an object has subjective value, its objective value may be unimportant. Instead—and once again—the *emotions* of interested bidders may dominate what happens. Emotions can drive the bidding sky-high, giving great pleasure to owners and auctioneers and great displeasure to other collectors. Indeed, museums lament the recent escalation in the price of important artwork. Current bids make it almost impossible for them to compete for the better pieces. Their acquisition budgets, which in previous years seemed fairly substantial, now can be less than the price of a single piece of art.

Even when there is no strong emotional attachment to the object, auctions still hype people's emotions. If you've ever attended an antique, a household, or an art auction, you know what I mean. Experienced, professional bidders don't get so excited. Instead, they do considerable research prior to an auction; they know which of their clients might be interested in which objects, and they bid quite rationally. But the first few times you attend an auction and decide to bid on something, you can feel your excitement build as you make your bids and other people bid against you. Even experienced bidders feel that way when the object is important.

Several years ago I attended a country auction with some friends. I was particularly taken by an old veterinarian's bag. I didn't need it, but it was enticing nevertheless. Two of my friends were tempted by the same rocking chair. Before the bidding began, we planned our strategy. We didn't want to bid against one another, so my friends had to decide who wanted the chair more. Anne was willing to bid as much as $60 and Bill wasn't, so the decision was easy. I set my limit for the bag at $5.

We all felt armed and ready. Anne asked if I would bid on the chair for her since she was really nervous. I said I would, but only if she gave me explicit instructions. She said I should keep bidding up to $60 and then stop.

My bag came up early in the bidding, but not by itself! An old doctor's bag had gotten no bids, so the veterinarian's bag was auctioned off with it. For $3 I got both bags. I had no interest in the doctor's bag, but this is one of the prices you pay at a country auction—you sometimes end up with things you don't want.

When the chair came up, I did my duty and entered bids for it. I frequently turned to Anne to make sure I should continue bidding. Someone behind us continued to bid as well. Finally, we made the winning bid—it was exactly $60. Afterward I couldn't help thinking that the owner of the rocking chair may have overheard us and pushed the bidding up to Anne's limit.

It's a lot like the story my barber recently told me. He was interested in buying a small cabin on a lake and overheard someone else expressing interest, too. He followed them to a tavern where they stopped for lunch. He sat nearby and overheard them discussing what they were going to offer. When he submitted his own offer, he was very well informed about what it should be! And he is now quite happy with his new vacation home.

THE WINNER'S CURSE

Other aspects of auctions can also stimulate people's emotions. I frequently run a simple auction that is designed to *reduce* emotions. I have a half-gallon Crown Royal bottle that's full of pennies; everyone makes a single, written bid for the contents. I have counted the pennies (*not* one at a time, as someone always suggests); the highest bidder gets paid in dollars and cents, not in pennies.

Everyone submits a bid in writing. People who don't want to take part in the auction can submit a ridiculously low bid, reducing their chances of being the winner (but keeping their payoff quite high if they do win). There is also a small prize for the best estimate of how many pennies are in the bottle.

Most people make safe bids: Neither their estimate nor their actual bid really approaches the value in the Crown Royal bottle, which holds just over sixteen hundred pennies. In two recent auctions for groups of about sixty people each, some bids approached the total, but only one bid in each group exceeded $16. One was $18 and the other was $32. The $32 bid is a great example of *the winner's curse,* where the person who wins an auction has paid more for the object than its objective value.

Research results indicate that (1) people often underestimate the value of what's being auctioned; (2) they usually bid less than their estimates; and (3) someone (the highest bidder) typically bids more than the object's value. This is even true for experienced bidders. When there are more than a handful of bidders (that is, more than five), odds are good that the winner will be cursed.

That people's bids are less than their estimates makes sense. High estimates can't cost you anything, but high bids can. The amazing result, however, is the frequency of the winner's curse. Winners are only cursed, though, with respect to objective values. When they also have subjective value for the prize, they may not feel cursed when they win, even when bids go very high.

SELLER STRATEGIES

If you are in the happy position of being the only producer and seller of some item or service, how can you sell your production for the absolute maximum?

If you are producing many of these objects, it's best to set a price determined by your costs and your customers' valuations. If you only have a few pieces, though, you should conduct an auction. The kind of auction depends on whether the bidders are risk averse (that is, they tend to play it safe) and whether they use each other's bids in evaluating the object's value. If bidders aren't particularly risk averse (they sometimes go for broke) and make up their own minds about the object's value, you should set a reserve price reflecting your own value for the object. Then any type of auction will work about as well as any other.

If the bidders are risk averse, a Dutch auction is best. You can imagine how concerned they will be as the price drops lower and lower. To avoid the risk of losing out, a risk averse bidder won't be able to wait.

If the bidders are uncertain about the object's worth, they may depend on each others' bids to get an idea of its value. They won't know ahead of time what they should bid. In this situation, English auctions should push them to higher bids, since the excitement and the information they get from everyone else should be encouraging.

You should always get as many bidders together as you can, and, if people are making their bids in writing, you should also let them know that there are many other bidders. Bidding can be in person, where everyone (or their agents) must be physically present, or by sealed bid. With my Crown Royal bottle, for instance, everyone could see the size of the group and everyone made sealed bids. If the bidding had been verbal rather than in writing, the unusually high bid of $32 would probably never have surfaced. The high bidder would only have had to beat the next highest bidder, who, according to their written (sealed) bids, offered less than $16. Thus, I might have lost money if I had held an open, verbal English auction.

Cartels, or bidding rings, sometimes organize themselves to avoid competition among themselves (just as my friends did before Anne bought the rocking chair). In professional cartels, one member of the group bids, and the group reauctions the prize later among themselves. The difference between the two winning bids is divided among the ring's members. Sellers can foil a cartel by setting a sufficiently high reserve price so that the cartel's in-group profits disappear. Or, if they have enough information, they can have an agent push the bidding up.

CONCLUSIONS

But if you're a bidder rather than a seller, how can you avoid the winner's curse? There is no clear answer to this question. People with experience in the Highest Number Game may bid less on subsequent games. And there are almost always incentives to collude, even though collusion can be hard to organize. Without collusion, the temptation to choose a higher number than the last game's winner is always present. Thus, bids might not drop much, even with experience.

In addition, recent research suggests that the winner's curse may be particularly impervious to learning. Thus, the best recommendation we can safely make is to be careful at auctions. Know how much your top bid will be before you start bidding, and don't let anyone know what it is. Get as much information as you can if the object has only objective value for you. And if it has subjective value, consider the other opportunities you might not have if you actually win the auction. Finally, try not to get too excited until the auction is *over*.

CHAPTER 12

SOCIAL
DILEMMAS

Imagine that you are nearing the finish of a two-day seminar on bargaining. Your professor has handed out blank envelopes to all forty of you. It is the last exercise in the seminar; it's your last chance to do well.

The rules for what she has called the Game of Envelopes and Money are simple. You can put any amount of money you wish in your envelope. If the total of all the money in the envelopes exceeds $250, you each get $10. You cannot discuss what you are going to do; everyone must decide for herself how much to put in the envelope. Whatever you contribute, your professor will keep the contents of the envelopes. If the total is over $250, she will pay everyone $10 each; if it's less, no one gets anything. How much would you put in your envelope?

THE DUTCH FIASCO

My first exposure to this game came at the end of an international conference on cooperation and social dilemmas. Almost fifty scholars from around the world had gathered in the Netherlands to hear each other's research. Clearly, it was a very well-informed group.

At our last session, David Messick and Christel Rutte presented us with the Envelopes and Money Game. Everything was as I've described it, except the currency was Dutch guilders rather than American dollars. That meant that the stakes were cut in half (making it more appropriate for a group of academics).

No one had been forewarned about this game. Many of us were leaving the Netherlands soon and had used as much of our Dutch money as we could. But, then again, Dave and Christel weren't asking for much.

First off, we all tried to get a good count of how many people were in the room. Although no one was sure of the exact number, there were actually forty-three people there, plus Dave and Christel. Many of us calculated what an equal share would be; we put that, plus a little—a "cushion"—in our envelopes. We figured that most contributions would be six or seven guilders.

It seemed like the counting took forever. Finally, the total was announced—245.59 guilders. We were stunned. As a group, we buzzed and exclaimed, trying to figure out how that could have happened. We had fallen short by less than 5 guilders.

STRATEGIES

Several factors that most of us didn't consider contributed to the outcome. Afterward, most people claimed that they had contributed six or seven guilders. Actually, only eighteen people did, and most of them contributed 6, not 7. Eight people contributed 10, as they had no small change. Four others only had small change and contributed all of it, but many of these contributions were 5 guilders or less. Seven people contributed nothing. All of them correctly predicted that the 250 guilders would not be reached, so they decided not to throw their money away. Five others predicted that the total would not be achieved, but they contributed something anyway, although it was less than 5 guilders each.

On the bus ride back to the hotel, several people claimed that they fully expected us to win, but that (1) they had no cash with them at all or (2) they had no change. The actual contributions, however, don't support their stories. Possibly it was an easy way to say that they had contributed when in fact they hadn't. Thus, for want of just one more optimist, we failed. In fact, if one of the seven who had predicted that we would fall short had, instead, contributed an equal share and predicted that we would get just over 250, we would have made it. Just one. This is another, powerful instance of a self-fulfilling prophecy.

Prior to the game, Dave had told me that I could have a real impact on the game if I wanted to. He didn't specify how, as he didn't want to reveal the nature of the game. Now I wish that I had contributed much more, even if it did mean a personal monetary loss. The money was not that significant. Instead, to be able to turn the tide for such a large group—and make him pay—that would have been very satisfying.

But none of us thought of contributing a lot. We were convinced that everyone would contribute their fair, equal share. Everyone was going to act as we did; things would work out very well. In essence, we overconcluded on the basis of our own point of view—we paid the penalty for our *egocentric bias*. We simply didn't see that some people wouldn't react exactly the way we did.

One obvious solution in this game is the short-term solution to a prisoner's dilemma game: Don't cooperate. Although you may do well by cooperating, it's risky. Also, if everyone contributes enough anyway, you win the prize and don't risk losing anything by contributing yourself. If everyone doesn't contribute enough, you don't gain but you don't lose either. And since your contribution is anonymous, you can tell any story you like on the bus.

Then why did I and many of my colleagues contribute? Our separate but similar egocentric biases were strengthened by being at the conference together and thinking that everyone understood how social dilemmas could be solved cooperatively if everyone pitched in. We were all familiar with an equal-share solution, where everyone shouldered the same risk and would gain about the same profit. Thus, the equality norm, which is quite pervasive in Western society, was another element that contributed to our choice of how much to contribute.

Seeing a good thing, I have run this game several times since that first experience. I have varied the amounts of money involved, but they have all been pretty similar to the games described here. Every time, people fail to contribute enough, even though most expect the total to be achieved. In fact, they tend to contribute much less than we did in Holland, and end up quite far from winning.

This result is discouraging: Can't people learn to contribute enough to attain a public good (that is, something that they can all share in)? Groups who fail at the task once usually don't want to try it again. When they do, they tend to contribute even less. One strong conclusion, then, is that this game is not conducive to cooperation. Indeed, a wide range of research has documented the difficulty of generating cooperation in large group dilemmas.

THE MOLLUSKS

An old friend who has been living in Brooklyn recently returned to Urbana for a few days. We were all interested in his latest "New York stories." Tim told us about his neighbors, a family he calls the Mollusks. The Mollusks are longtime residents of Tim's neighborhood; they are a family whose numbers are quite large. In addition to being a visual blight, they always seem to be renovating their home. One recent project, to redo their old concrete patio, presented them with a real problem: how to dispose of the chunks of concrete. The garbage service wouldn't haul them away and they didn't want to have to take them to the dump themselves.

Luckily a solution presented itself. One of the many problems of congested New York is abandoned cars. It so happened that someone had abandoned a car across the street from the

Mollusks' house. The authorities had inspected the car (which by this time had no tires, no battery, nothing removable still attached) and put an orange sticker on it, indicating that it would be hauled away for junk if the owner didn't remove it within forty-eight hours.

Well, the Mollusks put the big chunks of concrete in plastic garbage bags and loaded the bags into the car. They were relieved of their problem, but the car now weighed about eight tons.

When the city's abandoned-car remover arrived, it grabbed the roof of the car and tried to lift it onto a stack of about six cars it was already carrying. The driver's view of this new addition to his collection was blocked while he was working the crane, so he couldn't see that the roof of the car was rising, but the rest of the car wasn't. The car's roof supports were being stretched like chewing gum and were straining mightily. The driver soon realized his problem and gave up the task. Eventually, after many weeks, the city sent people out to unload the car and then, finally, haul it away.

But this wasn't the only problem the Mollusks had to solve to complete their patio. They also had to dig up a lot of dirt and clay and, of course, they didn't know how to dispose of that either. So in true neighborly fashion, they dumped it in the gutter in front of their house and used a big wrench to turn on the fire hydrant at the corner. Water gushed out of the hydrant, washing the dirt and clay down the street, away from the Mollusks' house. Their problem was solved again. But their neighbors down the block were somewhat surprised when they found their cars stuck in a foot of mud when it hadn't rained for days.

When we take the prisoner's dilemma or the Gas Station Game and expand them to large groups, we get social dilemmas. If everyone cooperates, we all do well. If everyone defects, we all do badly. And if most of us cooperate and some defect and free-ride, as the Mollusks do, the rest of us pay their costs. The Game of Envelopes and Money, described at the start of this chapter, is one of many examples of social dilemmas.

The classic story about social dilemmas is Garrett Hardin's "The Tragedy of the Commons." Near the center of most towns in seventeenth-century England was a common area that everyone could use. Picnics, county fairs, and summer weddings often took place there. Early on, there were no rules about the commons: Everyone in town could use it in any way they pleased.

Unfortunately, a herdsman realized that he could expand his herd without having to buy more land if he grazed his cows there. That way he could make the most of his own farmland and maximize his returns on his now larger herd. After he started doing this, the other herdsmen in town realized how profitable it could be, and they began to graze their cattle there, too. Before long the commons was reduced to a barren field, with no grass and no attraction for anyone or any social activity. No one even thought of getting married there anymore. As Hardin put it: "Ruin is the destination toward which all men rush, each pursuing his own best interest in a society that believes in the freedom of the commons. Freedom in a commons brings ruin to all."

The temptation to use a public good like the commons for personal gain is not unusual. The difficulty comes when one person's use interferes with others who also have a legitimate claim. Thus, just as the players in prisoner's or social dilemmas are dependent on each other's choices, so too are the people who share the commons.

Hardin used the tragedy of the commons to argue that people must submit to "mutual coercion, mutually agreed upon." He suggested that we must legislate ourselves so that no one will infringe on the rights of others and everyone can be better off. Clearly, then, the issues raised by prisoner's and social dilemmas can be quite significant when we extend them to more global, societal interactions.

SOCIAL DILEMMAS

We face a number of social dilemmas all the time. Consider the following examples.

1. The West Coast of the United States suffers another

drought. Up and down the coast, communities and towns enact voluntary restrictions on water consumption. The slogan "Save water, shower with a friend" becomes very popular. If everyone cuts down, they might not run out of water. But what about the choice a single person must make: What impact can he have on the entire system? An extra shower here or there won't hurt much and, after the heat of the day, a shower can really feel good. No one will know; it can be a completely private act. How, then, do you stimulate social responsibility so that less water is used?

This example describes a water shortage, but the principle is the same in any shortage situation, whether it is energy, food-stuffs, or animals in the wild. Hoarding scarce commodities or not protecting endangered species can increase personal benefits at the risk of serious societal losses. This is truly a *social* di-lemma; the solution is not obvious and large social groups are involved.

2. Charitable contributions provide another example. Will any single person's contributions to cancer research, for instance, increase their chances of being saved from its terrors if they contract the disease? Will thirty-five dollars from any individual save a local public television station? Will a donation to the Olympic team help someone break a world record and win a gold medal? In each case, the chances of an individual contribution having a direct impact on the hoped-for outcome is pretty unlikely. So why, then, would anyone contribute to cancer research, public television, or the Olympics?

3. Retail businesses sometimes have a choice about being open on Sunday. If there isn't enough business to cover the costs of staying open, most stores won't open, especially during the slow months of the year. But if only one of a group of competitors does, they will get all of that Sunday's business and their competitors will lose sales and customers. So once one store opens, the other stores will probably follow suit, and everyone will incur more costs than they should, just to make sure that someone else doesn't get ahead. Similar inefficiencies are produced by automobile rebates (once one company starts giving them, the others do, too, and everyone's profits drop), increases

in advertising (they don't improve the product but increase costs and stimulate unnecessary increases in advertising by everyone in the industry), and airline frequent-flier programs (no airline could let the others have this promotion without following suit—to their mutual detriment).

SOME SOLUTIONS

Charitable organizations play the persuasion/negotiation game constantly. By making their appeals attractive, by not asking for too much, and by appealing to potential contributors' emotions, they hope to induce cooperative responses from their audiences.

When people are asked to contribute to the needy, the hungry, or the homeless, the request is usually *personalized*. An ad might say: "Your contribution of $5 will feed a poor child for a week." If you do contribute, you will probably receive a personal note from a child (though probably not from the child who is receiving your contribution). Charities clearly think that this will increase the chance that you will contribute. As we will see, research results support this belief.

From a strictly rational, selfish point of view, however, noncooperation is a dominant short-run strategy, just as: (1) confessing was individually rational for the burglars in the original prisoner's dilemma story; (2) cutting your prices was best in the short run in the Gas Station Game; and (3) putting nothing in your envelope meant you couldn't lose anything and you might still win in the Envelopes and Money Game. Thus, the choices that individuals must make in a social dilemma are a lot like those in the dilemmas we've discussed in this book. Mutual cooperation can provide the larger group a tremendous benefit while individual noncooperation is tempting to everyone.

Nevertheless, everyday observations are much more encouraging. The Mollusks are unusual, hopefully an exception. People do vote, even when the chances of their vote making a difference are slim; they do contribute to public television and cancer research; they volunteer selflessly all the time. They do shower with a friend when voluntary water restrictions are needed. People solve dilemmas fairly well—not always, of course, and there are frequently a small number of scoundrels who poach or overconsume for their own profits. Thus, there is plenty of room for improvement. Recent research on social dilemmas identifies several factors that can help.

STRUCTURE AND PYSCHOLOGY

Solutions fall into two major categories: structural and psychological. The structure of any bargaining game limits the players' strategies and constrains possible outcomes.

Early work on cooperation showed that people are clearly affected by their outcomes. When the reward for mutual cooperation increases, so does cooperation. When mutual noncooperation is punished, cooperation also increases. When people know that they'll be interacting for a long time, they're more cooperative.

By changing the structure of an interaction in the right ways, then, cooperation can increase. When we think of the conflicts in the Middle East, a key element in Arab-Israeli negotiations is the structure of their interaction. When delegates are together at a bargaining table, one way to increase their chances for cooperation is to make sure that they decide to meet again. In addition, external influences like the United States or the United Nations can increase both parties' payoffs for cooperating or decrease their payoffs for noncooperating. These structural changes could increase cooperation—without even considering the psychological factors that also affect these negotiations.

People intuitively understand the power of structural changes. Research on the harvesting of scarce resources, for instance, shows that people who realize that they are overconsuming will relinquish some of their individual control so that a leader can keep everyone in line. Similarly, when people realize that voluntary cooperation is impossible, they may establish a punishment system that will ensure mutual cooperation. This mechanism is reminiscent of Hardin's suggestion of "mutual coercion, mutually agreed upon."

At least four psychological factors can contribute to increasing cooperation in social dilemmas: (1) individual values; (2) knowledge; (3) communication; and (4) group identity.

Values.   People can be categorized as having strong orientations toward cooperation, competition, altruism, or their own individual benefits. Cooperators try to maximize joint gain; altruists try to maximize others' gains; individualists are only interested in their own outcomes; and competitors pay most attention to whether they're doing better than someone else. Although we might hope that altruists and cooperators peopled the world (they have little trouble solving social dilemmas), true altruists are quite rare. But values can be provoked within a group: Presenting a lecture on the morals of contributing and playing fairly, for instance, can substantially increase cooperation.

Knowledge.   Knowledge about the other player and about the game itself can also help. When people expect others to cooperate, they become more inclined to cooperate, too. Also, people who know that noncooperation is dysfunctional in the long run often try hard to establish mutual cooperation. That way they can act cooperatively and expect cooperation in return. Observers of prisoner's dilemma games, for instance, are much more cooperative than the players they observe. Understanding that conserving resources early has long-run value also leads to more cooperation. Thus, although we often say that a little knowledge can be a dangerous thing, knowledge that highlights the value of cooperation can be particularly beneficial.

Communication.   In two-party prisoner's dilemmas like the Gas Station Game, communication does not always have a positive effect. In social dilemmas, however, the increase in the size of the group and the opportunity to communicate *before* people make their first choices can increase cooperation.

Communication (1) provides information about others' choices; (2) makes people think others are committed to cooperation; (3) allows people to raise moral arguments to influence others to choose cooperatively; and (4) increases a sense of group identity. Similarly, communication can raise ethical concerns that make it easier for people to do the right thing and cooperate. Explicit, personal pressure to cooperate has also been very effective.

Group identity. A common group identity or experiencing a common fate (which often provides a common identity) can also lead to more cooperation. People who identify more with each other cooperate more.

The positive effects of group identity may be due to (1) increased payoffs to smaller, tighter groups (since the payoff is spread over fewer people), (2) less chance that someone in the group will defect, (3) an increase in the importance of each person's actions, (4) less diffusion of responsibility, (5) greater pressures to conform, (6) in-group bias, (7) more fear of personal sanctions if you don't cooperate, (8) feeling that what's mine is yours and vice versa, and (9) the heightened responsibility you feel when you represent your group.

Internal group norms may also develop and contribute to cooperation. When people exhort each other to cooperate, they can be very effective, even when defecting has significant payoffs. In addition, publicizing choices—making people even more personally responsible for their actions—also leads to greater cooperation.

Emphasizing "we," that is, that group members will all experience a common fate, can significantly promote cooperation. Also, when you know you can make a difference, you are more likely to contribute. The same dynamics work here and in the volunteer dilemma. When someone knows that her contributions are critical for an entire group, she is more likely to pitch in.

The converse is also true: If you don't think you're going to be critical, you may not contribute. If someone else volunteers, you may not need to. Also, if your group's contributions won't be enough, there's no point in throwing your money away. However, the results of the Envelopes and Money Game are much less pessimistic. Even without believing that you are critical (only one person in the group in Holland thought he was), optimism and thinking that others would also contribute increased people's contributions.

CONCLUSIONS

As group size drops or as group identity increases, the impact of any single individual increases. Stimulating group identity, by having everyone share each other's company and recognize each other and their mutual dilemma, or by any number of other techniques, can increase cooperation tremendously. Thus, people who deal with each other socially as well as in business have an easier time cooperating on a deal: They have stronger personal ties and a stronger basis for trust and mutual cooperation.

The Mollusks, the herdsmen who graze on the commons, the free riders—each of them tend to act alone. Indeed, they may be social isolates. Being a true member of a group increases both identification and commitment. It can also increase cooperative contributions.

The choice to contribute to a group, any group, can be essential. Small companies survive because everyone pitches in and works overtime to keep things going; relationships flourish when both people contribute to each other; and international negotiators can only achieve arms reduction agreements if both sides are willing to take a chance with each other. All of these situations involve risks; in every case, you may lose your contribution, and more. But if no one contributed, no group would ever be able to survive. We would all have to go it alone—a daunting prospect.

CHAPTER 13

THE VALUE OF
INTEGRATING

You are in the market to buy a house. The neighborhood you're interested in has several attractive houses for sale. Let's assume that one broker is in charge of all sales, so you know you'll be bargaining with her for any house you might buy.

In preparing for negotiations, you realize that you have three major concerns: price, location, and closing date. Not surprisingly, there is a limit to how much you can spend. Thus, price is your first consideration. You would also prefer a house with a view or one near the creek that runs through the area. Although the closing date is your least important concern, you prefer to move later rather than sooner. All other issues except price can be easily worked out and aren't very important to you.

Let's simplify the situation and consider only nine possible prices, locations, and closing dates. The numbers associated with each price, location, or closing date, listed below, represent your priorities for the three issues. (The numbers are not essential for understanding the negotiations—the story is more important—but they can help structure your strategy. Thus, if you are inclined, you might try to determine your priorities in numerical terms before you begin a negotiation. If you don't like numbers, however, you can ignore them completely.) The essentials that are embodied in these numbers are the following:

(1) Price is most important to you; closing date is least important. (2) You would prefer to make a small concession (one level on the chart below) on price to a moderate concession (three levels) on location. (3) A small concession on price is more important to you than conceding everything on closing date; a small concession on location is also worth a big concession (five levels) on closing date.

Here are the actual numbers:

Prices	Value to You	Locations	Value to You	Closing Dates	Value to You
Very High	0,000	The Worst	0,000	Now	000
——	2,500	——	1,000	——	200
High	5,000	Fair	2,000	Soon	400
——	7,500	——	3,000	——	600
Moderate	10,000	Average	4,000	OK	800
——	12,500	——	5,000	——	1,000
Low	15,000	Good	6,000	Delay	1,200
——	17,500	——	7,000	——	1,400
Very Low	20,000	The Best	8,000	Later	1,600

You obviously would like to get everything: a very low price, the best location, and a later closing date. The numbers under the "Value to You" column are some measure of how happy you will be with each of the possibilities. If you buy the house for a very low price, you save $20,000. Getting the location you want most can't be expressed in money so easily, but it's less important than the price of the house. (We'll assume that the numbers have some relationship to dollars.) The same is true for closing date. The best you can hope for is a total of 29,600 (20,000 on price plus 8,000 on location plus 1,600 on closing date).

As you prepare for negotiations, you know that you simply

won't accept a deal unless you get at least 18,000. Anything worse than that means you should stick with your current living arrangements. In collective bargaining, this 18,000 minimum would be called your *resistance point*—you'll resist and won't accept anything less. You keep this number to yourself; it would be extremely valuable information for the other side.

With all this determined, you make an appointment with the broker. You have finished looking at houses. Now it's time to deal. You have no idea what the broker's priorities are, but you're pretty sure they won't be the same as yours. You don't really expect to get everything you want.

You meet with the broker and indicate your potential interest in several of the development's houses. She provides you with list prices. Just as you feared, good locations mean high prices. Next you ask about closing dates. Unfortunately, the news here also sounds bad. Sooner is uniformly better for the broker; all of the firm's houses are available immediately.

What happens next? Things appear pretty bleak. The broker's preferences are exactly the opposite of yours. You could get discouraged and give up, as some people do. Or you could hunker down and see if you could negotiate a lower price before you consider the less important issues. But both of these moves would be costly strategic mistakes, as we will see. Instead, let's consider an integrative strategy that is both simple and effective.

The first step is to see whether an agreement is even possible. If the situation is strictly competitive, it will take a lot of concessions by both you and the broker to reach agreement. That could mean a long, painful negotiation. But even if she prefers selling you a house with a high price in a bad location as soon as possible, her preferences may not be the *exact* opposites of yours—which means there's room to integrate. For whatever reason (for example, a loan coming due soon combined with a shortage of cash), she may want a quick closing badly. In addition, she may be relatively unconcerned about locations. Let's assume that her outcomes from different price, location, and closing date combinations look like this:

Prices	Value to the Broker	Locations	Value to the Broker	Closing Date	Value to the Broker
Very High	20,000	The Worst	2,000	Now	16,000
——	17,500	——	1,750	——	14,000
High	15,000	Fair	1,500	Soon	12,000
——	12,500	——	1,250	——	10,000
Moderate	10,000	Average	1,000	OK	8,000
——	7,500	——	750	——	6,000
Low	5,000	Good	500	Delay	4,000
——	2,500	——	250	——	2,000
Very Low	0,000	The Best	000	Later	0,000

Higher prices are worth as much to her as low prices are to you. And, although you don't know this (because there is usually no way for you to find it out), she does have a strong preference for quick closings. Closing date is much more important to her than it is to you. She's least concerned about location.

She will still bargain hard to sell you a house with a high price. But she would prefer selling you a house at a lower price if she can do it right away. Of course, she is not likely to tell you that—it would give you an unnecessary bargaining advantage. But she will concede fairly easily on location. That means that you can trade off location and closing date: You can give in on dates, accepting something sooner, in exchange for a better location. That is good for you *and* it's good for the broker.

You have no information about her other potential sales, as she doesn't know whether you have other alternatives. Thus, just as you won't agree for anything less than 18,000, she may also have a minimum profit below which she won't go.

How can you get all this information, or bargain as if you had it? (Remember, I have cheated and told you what her outcomes would be; you would only rarely have a chance to see this information.) You can still discover that mutually beneficial trade-offs are possible *without* much initial information by taking a problem solving approach. And you can do this without discovering her firm's cash flow problems.

First, you can reveal that you would prefer a house with a nice location and a low price and that you would prefer to delay as long as possible before you move in. This is not very revealing—she probably expects it. It does tell her, however, that your preferences and hers are quite different. Before the broker reacts competitively, however, you might also say that you would like to explore some possibilities.

You realize that a house with a Moderate price in an Average location with a closing date that is just okay will not make you happy: It only provides you with a total of 14,800 (10,000 price plus 4000 location plus 800 closing date). You need at least 3,200 more (to reach 18,000) to be happy with a deal.

You also know, however, that she may use this middle-of-the-road agreement as an anchor to determine whether she has done well. So you keep in mind that, while you need to do better than this compromise agreement to be happy, the broker might, too.

You also know that you can concede on the closing date before conceding on anything else. That is important. If you can get her to concede on price or location in exchange, you'll be on your way toward an *integrative* agreement where you both do well.

So you indicate to the broker, first, that you realize that the best location at a very low price with a perfect date may not be possible. Instead, you suggest some *hypotheticals*. For instance, would she prefer (1) a sale at a Very Low price with an Average location and a Later date to (2) a sale also at a Very Low price but with the Best location and an okay date? You prefer the latter (yielding 20,000 plus 8,000 plus 800 = 28,800) to the former (20,000 plus 4,000 plus 1,600 = 25,600). But what about her?

She won't accept either possibility—but they weren't real offers, just hypotheticals. Instead, you can ask which she prefers and whether her preference is strong. Her response to those two

hypothetical possibilities can be very revealing. If her preferences are the same as yours (that is, she prefers the second to
the first), you will know that you're on the right track. If she
prefers the first alternative, you need to try again with a different set of hypotheticals.

Let's say she clearly prefers the second alternative, just like
you. That is good news—a trade-off is possible. Her clear preference also signals that your concessions on closing date are valuable to her, even though they are not very costly for you. If
you asked her whether a Very Low price with a Good location
and Delay in the closing date was clearly better than the original, rejected first choice (a Very Low price with an Average
location and a Later date), she would probably say yes. That
would confirm to you that closing date was clearly more important to her than location. Now you know that you can get
more on location by giving on closing date, which is a very good
trade-off for you. If you can move one level later in closing and
get one level better on location, you can concede 200 to get
1,000.

Next you might see how she reacts to price and closing date
trade-offs by asking if she prefers (1) a Very Low price with an
Average location and Delay in the closing date or (2) a Low
price with an Average location and a Later closing date. She
might respond by saying that both possibilities are awful but that
she has a slight preference for the second. That tells you that
her preferences for price and closing date changes are fairly similar, with price more important. For you, however, one change
in price is worth a huge change in closing dates.

The picture is now fairly clear. By judiciously conceding on
closing date—which costs you very little but gets you a lot—she
should concede almost as much on price and a great deal on
location. What, then, can you expect from a final agreement?

Ultimately, you expect to concede everything on closing date
in exchange for concessions on location and/or price. If you assume that her value for price is similar to yours (that is, that a
dollar is a dollar for everyone), you may not expect to do better
than a Low price with the Best location (for a total of 23,000),
giving up everything on closing date. Getting a Low to Very

Low price and a Good location would be even better (23,500), but getting such a good price may not be realistic. Thus, you will probably have to concede some on price to get a better deal on location. Also, if the negotiations dictate that you settle for a Moderately Low price, you will still do very well if you get the Best location (20,500).

You can and should pursue these various possibilities, always as hypotheticals (unless for some reason the broker seems very interested in a combination that is very good for you), for as long as she is willing. The more hypotheticals she reacts to, the more information you get about her preferences. When she's fed up with hypotheticals, you can move into serious offers and say that you are not averse to some extended negotiations. You might start by offering a Low price at the Best location with a Delay. She says that that is way off; it's nowhere close to being acceptable. She may counteroffer, however, with a High price and an Average location Now. You could counter with a Low price at the Best location with an okay date. Her response might be a High price with a Good Location Now. During the negotiations you complain about her demands for a High price and her reluctance to offer better locations; she may respond with noises about your Low price and your insistence on more time until closing. At the same time, you both can make concessions that reduce your own outcomes only a little while providing concessions that are valuable to the other person.

Your next offer is again for a Low price with the Best location, with closing between okay and Soon. She responds with a High price at the Best location Now. You tell her you will accelerate the closing date if she comes down on price. She agrees to move to a Moderately High price for closing Now. You agree to closing Now only if she will move to a Moderately Low price. That is a concession of 600 for you to get her to come down 7,500 in price. She gains 6,000 in closing date and can close the deal (for a total concession of 1,500). She agrees. That gives you an outcome of 20,500; hers (which you don't know) is 23,500. Those outcomes are better than the middle-of-the-road agreement of Moderate price, Average location, and OK closing date *for both of you.* You give up everything on your least important issue (closing date); she gives up everything on hers (location).

Both of you do well: Together you take all of the integrative potential that's available in the game. Your outcome is not as good as hers, but you would almost never know that in a real negotiation. We also don't know her resistance point. If she didn't change it during the bargaining, we know that it was less than 23,500. If it was not much less, then this is clearly the best agreement you could reach. You should be very pleased.

An even simpler way to get to this same result is to reveal your preferences—but that depends on the two of you trusting each other quite a lot. You don't have to reveal particulars; you can be general and say, for instance, that you have a strong preference for keeping the price as low as possible and that you might be flexible on the other issues. She might then do the work and present you with hypothetical offers, rather than you having to do it. Or she may reciprocate your information sharing and reveal that she is more interested in the closing date than the location, but that she can't do a lot with price. These general revelations allow both of you to exchange productive offers right away, without having to use hypothetical possibilities first.

Most people aren't so effective. They quickly discover that their preferences and their opponent's appear to be complete opposites. Some people give up right away. Others shift quickly into a competitive mode: They negotiate hard, concede little, and hope that the other party will do most of the conceding. This usually leads to intense competition, even if the other bargainer wanted to be cooperative. While they're both competing with each other, rather than exploring and problem solving, they won't discover their possible trade-offs. They may ultimately agree, but only grudgingly.

Many people playing the Multiple Issues Game start by asking for their best possible outcome (for example, a Very Low price in the Best location). That is not a problem by itself. Unfortunately, some people take offense when their counterpart also asks for everything. This is the bargaining double standard: People criticize others for exhibiting the behavior they've just displayed. The double standard can also lead two bargainers into a competitive spiral. Instead, more rational bargainers see such extreme opening offers as preliminary checks that help determine whether the two parties actually do have opposing interests.

Some bargainers are inclined to be cooperative but restrict their negotiations to one issue at a time. That makes the discovery of trade-offs impossible. Although dealing with multiple issues simultaneously makes negotiations more complex, it's worth the effort and gives you a chance to find effective trade-offs.

Few bargainers recognize the subtle signal behind an opponent's initial concessions. Most people get too emotionally involved to realize that the other's first concession will probably be on the issue that he can concede most easily. Compounding this problem is the frequent practice of switching concessions to a different issue rather than making repeated concessions on the same issue. Conceding several times on the same issue emphasizes that someone can concede easily on that issue, but people just don't bargain that way.

If a buyer concedes once on closing date, for instance, and that doesn't get her far, there's no reason to prematurely switch and concede on location or price. By doing so, she makes a greater concession than she needs to while simultaneously reducing the chance for subtly indicating to the opponent that closing date is her least important issue. She may feel that she hasn't gotten much from her first concession, so she concedes *more* on the next round. But however natural this strategy is, it's wrongheaded. A series of smaller concessions on your least preferred issue is much more effective, and can pave the way for fruitful integration.

Some people actually discuss their priorities. They simply ask each other, "Which issue is most important to you?" When they're both truthful, they have an easy and successful negotiation and avoid the aggravation of either competitive bargaining or the grudging, difficult process of making one concession after another.

Being able to discuss your priorities and work toward a problem-solving bargaining style takes considerable experience and *trust*. Before you begin negotiations, you may not know whether you can trust the other person. Even then, however, it pays to leave that possibility open. There are people who give others the benefit of the doubt and trust them right away; they do it automatically. Experienced bargainers, on the other hand, learn how to keep the opportunity for trust open without exposing themselves to serious danger.

GOALS

Another aspect of the Multiple Issues Game contributed to many people's final outcomes. The complete-compromise, middle-of-the-road agreement would not have satisfied you—it falls short of your 18,000 goal. As a result, you wouldn't accept a Moderate price at the end. Having a specific, difficult goal actually puts you in a better bargaining position at the end.

You will disagree if the broker can only achieve her goal at a Moderate price—but you can't know this ahead of time. Indeed, you may waste a lot of time and effort if no agreement is possible. But you should not always expect to reach agreement. (This is another of bargaining's basic truths. A good analog is one of the rules of thumb in the game of bridge: You know you are bidding well when about 20 percent of your contracts fail.) If you set your goals too high, you will never agree. But if your goals are reasonable—based on how you want to feel when the negotiations are over and on what you know about the market—you will get better outcomes and you won't agree unless you're happy with what you're getting. Even when you are bargaining well, disagreements are bound to happen. And some agreements are *worse* than no agreement at all (for example, the winner's curse).

In addition to a goal or resistance point, labor-management negotiators also establish a *target* before they begin bargaining. It identifies what they realistically hope to achieve. Targets are much less rigid than resistance points: As the negotiations proceed, most bargainers realize that they will probably not get as much as they hoped for. Establishing targets and resistance points structures the negotiation and allows you to know how well you're doing, both during and after the negotiations. If you don't establish targets and resistance points ahead of time, you can convince yourself that you got a good deal when you didn't—or when you shouldn't have reached an agreement at all.

Research has repeatedly shown that bargainers who have goals or resistance points do better than bargainers who don't. Goals help negotiators to bargain hard, and by bargaining hard—not competitively, not unethically, but professionally—they increase the chances that they will do better and that they will drain all the integrative potential from their negotiation.

MULTIPLE ISSUES

When we think about bargaining, like buying a car, we typically think about haggling over a single issue—price. The problem with this kind of thinking, as we have seen, is that we often focus on that one issue and don't think of including other issues in the deal. By including two or more issues in a negotiation, we can change the entire character of a negotiation. In fact, the importance of this structure—where two negotiators bargain over two or more items—is hard to overestimate. A big part of the old couple's problem in the Battle of the Sexes was that they were only in town for *one* final night. Multiple items make trade-offs possible, and trade-offs give both sides the opportunity to do better individually and collectively. Trade-offs allow people to *integrate,* to discover a solution that simultaneously satisfies everyone's most important priorities. Bargaining is most effective when people integrate and take advantage of trade-offs. It's what people mean when they talk about win-win bargaining.

"I'll give you this if you give me that" is the key message in integrative bargaining. This immediate reciprocity is not possible when people bargain over a single item. But just as completely competitive interactions are rare, so too are situations that must be limited to a single issue. Take two people who have a long-term relationship. They can almost always provide themselves with trade-offs by making sure that they never negotiate just one issue. They can include a future deal they know they'll be confronting anyway. Thus, when a wife and husband are trying to determine where they will go on this year's vacation, and the wife loves the mountains and her husband loves the beach, they can solve the dispute by deciding to go to the mountains now with the promise that they will go to the beach next year (or vice versa). Head-to-head, competitive bargaining can almost always be avoided by expanding negotiations to include more than one issue.

Understanding how trade-offs can work, knowing to look for them, and protecting yourself from obstinately competitive opponents are important bargaining skills. People often think that bargaining necessarily means competition. The unfortunate consequence of this kind of thinking is that it leads to their acting competitively, which pushes the other bargainer into a competitive mode too. People can hope for cooperation but fall into the trap of reacting competitively. They will then treat multiple issues the same way they treat single issues, by coming on strong and bargaining competitively. They won't explore the possibilities; they'll simply dig in their heels and try to influence the other person to concede. When the other person reciprocates, things can get hostile. Both sides lose, interpersonally and monetarily (if money is involved).

Almost all negotiations have room for *problem solving*. By switching gears and viewing bargaining as a problem solving task rather than one where you must beat the other person, you can discover trade-offs and integrative solutions that serve everyone very well—especially you.

As we've seen, totally competitive games are rare. Almost all games mix cooperation and competition simultaneously. When people take advantage of the cooperative aspects of a game and protect themselves from its competitive side, they do quite well. In addition, they can help their fellow bargainers do well, too. That requires a problem solving rather than a strictly competitive frame of mind, tempered with caution. The strictly cooperative strategy is risky: If you act cooperatively and others act competitively, you may lose a lot. A strictly competitive strategy, on the other hand, loses the potential benefits of mutual cooperation. From the simple standpoint of efficiency, however, almost every interaction offers joint gains that the negotiators, if they're good, can discover and exploit. This is the yin and yang of bargaining, the hope that cooperation will flourish, opposed by the fear that things will become unnecessarily competitive—and costly.

STRATEGIES

Let's consider again the bargaining game of buying a used car. Often that is a negotiation focused only on price. But adding issues—complicating the game—makes trade-offs possible. When you're buying from a dealer, you can ask for a guarantee and, in the process, establish the opportunity for trade-offs that will improve both of your outcomes. If the dealer won't come down on price, he may be able to extend the guarantee period. You get the assurance that the car will work for longer than you might have originally expected; he gets a sale at a price that might have turned you away.

Dealing with a private individual is harder. Issues like a guarantee are not usually part of a private sale. But you *can* inquire about sharing the costs for the repairs that will be needed to get the car into top running condition. Then you can bargain over the selling price and how much each of you will pay for the repairs. If you know you'll be making those repairs anyway, you can increase the chances of an integrative agreement—one that reduces your overall costs, provides you with a used car in tip-top shape, and gives the seller a reasonable price.

Bargaining takes advantage of these trade-offs when you both combine "gives" and "gets." Every time you make a concession (a "give"), you should also "get" something in return. That is the essence of effective integrative bargaining.

What do you do, though, when your opponents are totally unyielding? They only consider one issue at a time, making an integrative solution impossible. They simply stonewall and demand that you concede before they will do anything.

The only realistic solution if you want to reach an agreement is to be equally stubborn in pushing trade-offs. Repeatedly offering different trade-offs will break down just about anyone. It's similar to the strategy used by Henny Youngman, the old comedian who tells lousy jokes. He readily admits that his jokes are awful, but he has so many of them, sooner or later you have to laugh.

If time is important to you and you need to complete a deal in a hurry, an intractable opponent is a real pain. The old saying "Everything comes to one who waits" has an equally appropriate converse: "If you can't wait, you can't win." That is not always true, but exceptions are rare. If you are not pressed for time, being dedicated to integration will usually work. It may take considerable effort and a lot of time, but trade-offs can almost always be discovered. You won't always be successful at integrating. But, over many negotiations, dedicated integrators do very well.

CONCLUSIONS

There's nothing wrong with bargaining hard. Exploratory hard bargaining is really the key here—pushing for what you can find rather than simply following a win-win-win, concede-as-little-as-possible, competitive strategy.

Trust helps a lot. In familiar settings, where we have even a small indication that trust is possible, information sharing can be very constructive. Indeed, by revealing truthful information yourself, you invite the other party to be trustworthy and you increase the chances for integrating. Trust, however, is very fragile. Violating each other's expectations—expectations that are rarely communicated explicitly—can quickly overturn a relationship that is progressing toward integration. This fragility makes an integrative-competitive shift a constant danger. And if things do shift and trust is broken, it is very difficult to resurrect.

The moral of this chapter is that a foundation of trust is not absolutely necessary to take full advantage of a bargaining game's integrative potential, but it sure helps. Both parties can be better off. So why ignore outcomes that are better for everyone involved—if you can achieve them? If you can trust other people, they may reciprocate and trust you. If the negotiations are sequential (one person makes a move before the other), you can also increase the chances of reciprocal trust and integration by making small, safe cooperative moves early in your negotiations.

To sum up, looking for integrative potential can be very beneficial. If you can't find it (it's almost always there), you might be able to create some by adding an issue that will require negotiation in the future anyway. In the end, you might be able to make life better for everyone. So integrate!

CHAPTER 14

FAIRNESS
AND ETHICS

One of your neighbors is about to sell his car. It's three years old and in reasonably good shape. He realizes that selling it himself gives him the best opportunity to get the highest price for it, but he's concerned for two reasons: It was involved in a major accident and it has a recurring oil leak. If he tells potential buyers about these problems, he'll turn them away. If he doesn't, he may be acting unethically. His alternative is to just trade the car in to the dealer, since then he won't have to worry so much about revealing its faults.

This common situation is one of many examples of a negotiation that forces a bargainer to make ethical decisions. Unfortunately, while some people see a questionable action as ethical, others see it as unethical. In addition, subtle changes in a situation can make a huge difference in ethical judgments. Selling to a dealer rather than to a private individual, for instance, relaxes many people's—including your neighbor's—ethical standards.

Other examples of difficult-to-resolve ethical dilemmas abound. Doing business on the Pacific Rim, for instance, may involve the exchange of what Americans think of as bribes, but which locals consider appropriate ways to complete a deal. If you are actually faced with this situation, do you do what's normal "over there," or do you do what's normal here and probably lose the deal?

Take another situation: You are looking for a job when times are tight. During your one and only interview, the company representative asks whether you are considering other positions. Some people find it perfectly reasonable to conceal their plight, and try to be vague, saying "I'm pursuing other possibilities." Others feel obligated to say that this is their only interview; they consider anything else deceptive and unethical.

Debates over what is and what is not ethical can become very heated, as exemplified in a recent public television series on ethics, in which reasonable, intelligent people often differed vehemently on their judgments of ethical and unethical behavior. Life would be much easier if we could draw a line and say that behavior on one side was ethical and behavior on the other was unethical. But that is impossible. Nevertheless, in the rest of this chapter, I will try to identify some of the behaviors in the bargaining games we have considered so far that I think are unethical. I invite you to disagree with my conclusions. It's important for society and its members not to be complacent about ethics. They are critical determinants of how we behave in all of our bargaining games.

REASONS WHY

People act unethically to serve themselves. Although considerations of others may come into play, most unethical behavior is associated with "me-first" motives. Competition and greed are two of the strongest drives to unethical behavior.

Amazingly, people sometimes act unethically even when ethical behavior would have been just as effective. Thus, uncertainty is another driving force. For instance, even though expert observers unanimously agreed that Richard Nixon would win the 1972 United States presidential election, the Watergate burglars nevertheless engaged in illegal and unethical acts that were prompted, at least in part, by a desire to ensure his victory.

I'd like to propose one rule of thumb for selecting a bargaining strategy: Consider a variety of different strategies and assess how effective they might possibly be; if ethical acts can work well, do what you can to make them truly effective. Extra effort to be ethical is personally rewarding in the short run and objectively rewarding for everyone in the long run.

A friend told me an important story that exemplifies this quite clearly. The University of Washington was building a major extension of their football stadium. Before the addition, it consisted of a large set of stands with a huge roof over the seats. Since Seattle was well known for frequent rain, the roof was quite important. Due to the success of the football program, the school decided to duplicate this large tier of stands on the other side of the stadium.

During construction, someone made a terrible mistake and newly installed beams collapsed. No one was seriously injured, but the financial costs were considerable. The next day, after some investigation, the president of the construction company held a news conference. He said that employees of his company had made the mistake, that he was very sorry that it had happened, that he was tremendously relieved that no one was hurt, and that his company would take responsibility for the accident. He explained that they might lose money on the project, but they felt that, with luck, they would still be able to finish construction near the expected completion date.

Could we have expected his explanation to go this way? We have all heard accounts that try to dodge the blame for chemical plant explosions and huge oil spills, just to pick two examples. Cover-ups and laying the blame elsewhere have almost become the norm rather than unfortunate exceptions. Thus, this construction company seems quite unusual. They actually took responsibility for their mistake. They didn't hide. They didn't try to explain it away. They didn't try to use the courts to reduce their liability.

The aftermath of this incident was a surprise for the company president: He had more offers for work than he could possibly handle. People with construction projects beat a path to his door, knowing that they would be hiring someone dependable. As he put it, this is a sad commentary on the current status of big business. It's also a good lesson in the objective value of ethical behavior.

FAIR TO ME VERSUS FAIR TO YOU

Another force that leads to unethical behavior is a negotiator's sense of justice. If you feel that someone has treated you fairly, it's much easier to treat her fairly as well. If you think that she has consciously deceived you or acted unethically, you may also feel compelled to respond in kind.

The problem with feelings of justice is that they aren't stable. An old theory of bargaining suggests that people choose strategies, consciously or unconsciously, to promote outcomes that favor them most. In the Midwest, for instance, bicycle riders rarely stop for traffic signals or for pedestrians. But when these same people are driving their cars or walking, they get upset when cyclists don't obey traffic rules or give them the right-of-way. People use cycling strategies when they are riding, they use pedestrian strategies when they're walking, and they act like any other driver when they're driving. The point is that people frequently choose strategies that give them the best outcome possible, even if they conveniently adopt inconsistent roles in different situations.

Perceptions of justice are particularly important when two people of unequal status and unequal inputs must divide a joint benefit. Let's assume that Jeanne and Diane are partners in a new company. Jeanne has contributed more capital and more expertise; Diane has been an integral part of the company but has contributed less capital and less expertise. At the end of their first year, they decide that their unexpected profits allow each of them a bonus. Jeanne suggests that the bonuses be proportional to their inputs and their investments. Since it's hard to measure expertise, she suggests that they divide the money in the same proportions as their initial capital investments. She is using the *equity* norm—outcomes should be proportional to inputs.

Diane proposes that they split the bonus money equally. She reasons that they were both necessary for the company to get off the ground and that, even though Jeanne contributed more, the company would have gone nowhere without her. She is using the *equality* norm.

Both norms are easily recognizable and societally acceptable. Unfortunately, they generate different distributions of the bonus money. It would be unusual for Jeanne and Diane to switch their arguments, especially if they are at all competitive. Instead, people tend to support their positions by choosing common norms that happen to give them their best outcome.

In other situations, where determining inputs is more ambiguous, the equity norm often has less pull. In many musical groups, for instance, the members all share their pay equally, even though some members of the group may be more important than others. Thus, some of the strength of Jeanne's argument comes from the fact that she could use an objective criterion, that is, her capital investments, to make her claims.

OTHER FORCES ON FAIRNESS

Other, more situational forces lead people to behave in ways that could be considered unethical or even against the law. Consider what happened after Hurricane Hugo hit Charleston, South Carolina, a beautiful southern town, in the fall of 1989. Electricity, water, and telephone service were out for weeks in many areas. A few enterprising merchants who had access to electricity and clean water sold ice to people in need. Some priced a bag of ice at two dollars; others charged ten.

The principles of supply and demand suggest that consumers should expect inflated prices. But is $10 a fair price for a bag of ice, even if people will pay it?

Research suggests that most people in this situation feel that $10 is unfair. People know what ice should cost: $2 is reasonable; $10 is not. For ice to cost much more, it needs to be for a good reason, like severely increased costs. Simply taking advantage of people is not ethical.

Another aspect of fairness concerns how decisions are made. For instance, people who get poor outcomes on the basis of someone else's decision don't always feel that they have been treated unfairly. Instead, we feel most unhappy when we would have done better if the decision maker had only used appropriate procedures. We aren't so quick to react if (1) our outcomes are reasonably good, (2) our outcomes are bad but changing the decision making procedures wouldn't have changed our outcome, or (3) we feel we're responsible for what we got. Some people who find that they've bought a lemon of a used car, for instance, will get mad at the person who sold them the car. Others will get angry at themselves, telling themselves they should have known better than to be so trusting.

Departures from what's reasonable and fair, then, can encourage unethical behavior. Used car salespeople, for instance, often complain about the way people treat them. A vicious cycle of unethical, unhappy bargaining can ensue, even before a particular car seller has had a chance to act either ethically or unethically.

VARIETIES OF UNETHICAL BEHAVIOR

There are lots of ways to be unethical. Below, I have ranked seven basic types of unethical behavior from least to most severe.

1. *Selective disclosure and/or exaggeration* is a common practice in used car (and other) negotiations. In the example at the beginning of this chapter, which had your neighbor selling a used car, his ethical dilemma was whether to reveal the car's defects. Like many car sellers, he may highlight, overemphasize, and extol the virtues of his vehicle. By failing to mention the negatives, he opens himself up to charges of deception. At the

same time, he can defend himself by saying that he answered all of a buyer's questions truthfully. If a buyer doesn't ask all the right questions, it isn't his fault. He wasn't dishonest. If the buyer is a friend or a relative, however—a slight change in the scenario—then not revealing becomes more questionable, regardless of the questions asked.

2. *Misrepresentation* involves deception concerning a person's target or resistance points. When your neighbor is asked to reveal the lowest price he would accept for his car, he misrepresents if he quotes a figure that is higher than his lowest acceptable price. But since this is a negotiation, and not a question about fact, his misrepresentation is ethically acceptable. He shouldn't have to reveal his lowest price—if he does, he'll sell the car for that amount, even when he could have reasonably sold it for more. On the other hand, if the prospective buyer had asked whether the car had been in an accident, saying no is a lie. It's more than misrepresentation; it's a misstatement of fact, and clearly unethical.

3. *False threats* include insincere statements about terminating the negotiation or the relationship. When we played baseball as kids, my brother frequently threatened to take his bat and go home when he disagreed with an important decision in the game. Unfortunately, his threats were not always false, which increased their effectiveness.

4. *Deception* gives other negotiators information that encourages them to make conclusions that aren't true—like implying that something will happen without actually saying that it will. If your neighbor gave possible buyers a photocopy of a section in *Consumer Reports* that said that his model car was very dependable, he would imply that his car was reliable, too. Knowing its history and its oil leaks, however, means that the photocopy is clearly deceptive. Cars like his may be dependable in general, but his particular car isn't. When it doesn't live up to expectations, a buyer will feel deceived even though what he expected was never actually promised. Your neighbor can tell him that it was his expectations that were incorrect, although that is an empty denial.

5. *False promises* offer a concession that is insincere. They

are the reason people should get everything in writing. If your neighbor promised that the car would run like a top—knowing that it wouldn't—he was being unethical. The problem here is the fine line between expecting something to go wrong and knowing that it will. Thus, an expert car mechanic may need to reveal much more about a car than an owner who doesn't know cars.

6. *Falsification* of factual information is an outright lie. There is a fine distinction among misrepresentation, deception, and lies. Victims tend to call any of them lies. Thus, if your neighbor's car breaks down after the sale, the buyers will probably think he lied to them. Ethically, however, falsifying information is much more severe than deception or misrepresentation. Here, almost all of the blame lies with the perpetrator.

7. *Inflicting direct and intentional harm* is the most severe form of unethical behavior on this list. If your neighbor sabotaged the car in a way that would only show up after the buyer had driven it for a while, that would be a serious breach of ethics. Severe extenuating circumstances are the only reason for concluding that he was not acting unethically.

The above ranking is not clear-cut. Deception, for instance, may not be worse than a false threat. I have listed them in this order because false threats are often so insincere that they aren't believed anyway. But the rankings are clearly arguable.

Many people say that the only morally acceptable course of action is to tell "the whole truth and nothing but the truth." Yet revealing the whole truth can be very difficult to achieve. Even in court, truthful witnesses are not always asked all of the questions that would allow them to tell the whole story. Instead, important questions may be missed, either advertently or inadvertently, and they don't get a chance to reveal all of the truth.

Telling the whole truth may be laudable, but it can also get you into big bargaining trouble. If you reveal the lowest price you would accept for your house, you will probably get it! And during the sale, when everyone understands that they are involved in a negotiation, misrepresenting such a critical, personal piece of information is expected. In this context, then, it may not be unethical.

EXCUSES

People construct a variety of excuses to rationalize why they have behaved unethically. Some of them include:

- "It was unavoidable." This is like the repeated statement by the Vicomte de Valmont in *Dangerous Liaisons:* "It's beyond my control." People blame the situation rather than themselves. That is often very convenient.
- "It was harmless." The extent of the injury inflicted is not perceived by the harm-doer. Of course, that individual is not feeling the pain he has caused.
- "I did it to avoid something even worse." In other words, the ends justify the means. Particularly when a deceptive act has social or political implications—for example, lying to the secret police about the hiding place of political refugees—this explanation is sometimes acceptable even to those who are deceived, but certainly not to the secret police.
- "I did it to provide a greater good." This is the flip side of the previous excuse. Unfortunately, it often has little justification: The greater good is frequently only for the deceiver.
- "In this situation, it was okay." This is like the cliché, "All is fair in love and war." Thus, while some players in the game of business feel that false promises are acceptable, others may take them as a firm commitment to act as promised.

THE OBEDIENCE EXPERIMENTS

In the early 1960s, Stanley Milgram's studies of the limits of authority caused a tremendous stir about ethics in experiments. In a typical session, he asked one person to act as the teacher and the other, actually his accomplice, as the learner. The teacher and the learner were seated in separate rooms. After hearing a list of word pairs, the learner had to recall the second word when he was prompted with the first. If he was wrong, the teacher was supposed to administer an electric shock. With each successive wrong answer, the experimenter directed the teacher to increase the voltage on a simulated shock machine. The readings increased by 15 volts at each step, from 15 to 450. Increasing levels of voltage had labels ranging from "Slight Shock" to "Danger" to "Danger: Severe Shock" to "XXXX."

The learner (accomplice) was never actually shocked. Instead, he played a tape recording that included a series of incorrect responses. At 300 volts, the learner yelled loudly and pounded on the wall, asking the teacher to stop, and complaining of a heart condition. Then he simply stopped responding. When teachers hesitated in administering additional shocks, the experimenter reiterated that they must continue, that the experiment required that they continue, that it was essential that they continue, that they had no other choice and they must go on, that there was no permanent tissue damage, that you must go on whether the learner likes it or not, and that no response should be treated as an incorrect response.

Afterward, people were informed about everything that happened and the purpose of the study. Nevertheless, the fact that no one stopped below 300 volts and that twenty-six of forty participants went all the way to the maximum 450 volts led observers to wonder whether people would be able to forget that they had engaged in behaviors that could have been seriously damaging to a fellow human being.

From our list of potentially unethical actions, Milgram certainly engaged in selective disclosure by not telling people ahead of time what was actually going to happen. He misrepresented by not revealing his intent. He clearly deceived people and implied false threats (for example, you must go on). He engaged in falsification by describing the shocks the learner would ultimately receive. But he didn't intentionally harm his subjects.

Social scientists continue to debate whether this study was ethical. Some argue that the deception and the experiences of the subjects were harmless; others claim that it provided a greater good (for example, increasing what we know about obedience and authority).

Introductory psychology classes often see a documentary film of the experiment. It is stark, black-and-white, and tremendously riveting. Early on, when the learner says "Ouch" to one of the shocks, almost everyone in the audience laughs. But by the time the teacher is administering the higher shock levels, it's clear that he is in great distress. Even in large classes, you can hear a pin drop. Everyone seems to be holding his breath. The drama is very compelling and the relief on the face of the teacher when he sees that the learner is okay makes the viewers sigh with relief, too.

SITUATIONAL CONTINGENCIES

Even a severe act like falsification can sometimes be judged ethical. Harboring political or religious refugees, for instance, and lying to the authorities who are pursuing them might seem acceptable—depending on your politics. If, however, you felt that the government's position was important and morally right, serious, disruptive dissension might need to be squelched. Thus, some people refer to acts like harboring fugitives as treason. In such circumstances, you would indict those who hid refugees and accuse them not only of unethical behavior but also of a very serious crime.

Thus, a particular set of values or a point of view may make one person's ethical behavior unethical to someone else. Clearly, then, we will find ourselves in very murky water if we begin arguing for the validity or morality of any particular point of view.

To begin, though, we can distinguish between interactions that are mutually defined as negotiations and those that aren't. For instance, as buyers at a flea market or an antique store or a used car lot, we know that we can negotiate the price of the object. We know that and the seller knows that. It may not be stated explicitly, but it's pretty clear. Similarly, when people hire a mediator to assist them in reaching a divorce agreement or when they hire a real estate agent to help them buy a house, they know that they are entering a negotiation.

When a teenager asks his parents to borrow their car, though, neither he nor his parents may think of their interaction as a negotiation. If he returns home with the gas gauge below empty, Mom and Dad might have reason to be angry. They might get even angrier if he says, "Well, I mowed the lawn for you yesterday." Since this was not defined as a negotiation, the concepts of reciprocity and quid pro quo become inappropriate.

Another situational distinction concerns the severity of the consequences of an act. An example is the justification that someone's actions "didn't hurt very much." It's often unclear how they would know how much hurt another person actually felt. Nevertheless, we might view the theft of an apple as less severe than the theft of a person's life savings.

All of this discussion indicates that we are rejecting a purely absolutist approach to ethics, that is, the view that an act that is wrong in one situation is equally wrong in another. At the same time, however, we don't espouse a purely relativist approach, which says that every action must be evaluated in its particular context. These are the two extremes. In between are extenuating circumstances, arguments for the acceptability of what might otherwise be unethical behaviors, and forms of deception that may be more or less ethical much of the time.

CONSEQUENCES

The consequences of unethical bargaining inflict themselves on the person who has engaged in the behavior, the other people in the situation (the victims), and society in general. Let's assume that the perpetrator recognizes his or her behavior as unethical. That is not always the case, of course. People sometimes don't realize that they have behaved unethically. And even when a victim or observer points it out, they may still feel they acted ethically.

If Jane is generally happy with herself as a person and feels that she has behaved ethically in an interaction she is replaying in her mind, her judgments about herself as a worthwhile human being are reinforced. She can tell herself she did the right thing, she was fair, she would act the same way again. Self-evaluations are easy when you feel you have acted ethically.

If Jane feels she has acted unethically, she will probably have feelings of regret and may attempt to undo her unethical behavior. If she can't correct the situation, she may suffer a loss of self-esteem. If she can try to remedy the situation, even if she's unsuccessful, the attempt may be enough to keep her self-image intact. Either way, unethical behavior provides her with negative consequences.

The recipients of ethical behavior may not only raise their evaluations of the ethical person, but they may also generalize their reactions to other people as well. Being able to trust one person can make it easier to trust others. The individual's reputation for being fair and ethical is strengthened and, to some degree at least, everyone benefits.

For victims, however, the downside is much worse. Just as bad news is more easily remembered and gets more attention than good news, *unethical behavior has much more impact than ethical behavior.* An unethical actor's reputation may be severely, even irreparably, damaged. Unethical behavior can also poison entire systems. Loss of trust in one person can put people on edge and make them hypersensitive to untrustworthy behavior by others. The wide-ranging negative reputations of used car dealers is a simple example: They have a very difficult time establishing credibility.

When someone realizes that he has acted unethically, his efforts to correct the situation must be emphatic. Even then, it's hard to erase people's memories. The consequences of unethical behavior can be tremendous and, in the long run, far outweigh potential gains. From a strictly pragmatic point of view, unethical behavior is just not worth it.

SOME EXAMPLES

Throughout this book, there have been instances of potentially unethical behavior in some of the negotiations. We'll go over several and discuss whether they are in fact unethical.

The rug in the Old City. The first instance comes in the Introduction, in my story of rug buying in the Old City of Jerusalem. I noted how my first negotiation, over the funky bag, indicated that I had to be careful. The bag seller tried to get me to think that the bag was older than it really was. I was forewarned. When the rug seller asked me how much I had paid for my rug and I told him $10, that was not the whole truth and nothing but the truth. As we know, I had paid $12 for the rug.

Was my statement unethical? Let's consider the context. First, what was the purpose of the seller's question? Was he trying to assess current market prices? I am pretty sure he wasn't. Although I have no evidence concerning how frequently he asked this question of people who walked by with rugs under their arms, I am still pretty sure he was not doing market research.

Was he trying to sell me another rug? I think he was. His actions toward me were very similar to those of other shopkeepers. He was very persistent—I should say relentless. He almost dragged me into his shop. He kept talking to me as I walked away. His actions suggested that he was trying to make a sale.

What about me? Was I bargaining? I didn't think so. I had absolutely no interest in buying another rug. I surprised myself by buying the first one. He couldn't have known that. To him I was probably just another consuming tourist, which was not altogether wrong. So while he may have been negotiating, I wasn't. I didn't realize at the time that I was collecting material for a book, but I certainly wasn't negotiating.

Finally, what were the rules for bargaining in the Old City? I observed all sorts of bargaining behavior, from serving potential customers mint tea (to soften them up?) to announcing repeatedly in a loud voice, "There is no cost in looking," to a young child saying what seemed like the only English words he knew: "Give me money. Give me money. Give me money." Merchants lied to me, tried to get me to offer a price, and always kept talking to try to keep me in their shops. Thus, I concluded that, from the sellers' point of view, outright thievery may not have been appropriate but the sharpest of bargaining tactics were acceptable and possibly encouraged.

In summation, I conclude that my statement was not unethical. Certainly this is a self-serving conclusion. But I have had little regret or remorse since then. I still think of this interaction as amusing, enjoyable, and totally harmless. What do you think?

The Blind Partnership Game. This game provided people with several opportunities to engage in unethical behavior. People with low numbers had a predicament: How could they split 50-50 with knowledgeable, experienced people who had high numbers?

Some people said that they had a high number when they knew it was low. That looks like an outright case of falsification and should be deemed unethical. But the situation has a lot to do with any final judgment we might make. Everyone knew they were negotiating; after the first play, everyone knew how to play the game; and everyone knew that those with high numbers should keep their own to do well. Thus, people could easily confirm an I-have-a-higher-number signal by proposing that both players keep their own.

If the person is falsifying, this proposal presents them with a real problem. If they accept, they're stuck with a low total; if they don't, they signal that they don't have a high number after all. Thus, regardless of anyone else's strategy, people with high numbers should have used keep-their-own strategies and been unaffected by anyone else's strategies.

This logic also applies to the *fait accompli* strategy, that is, acting as if you had a high number and the other person understands it, too. This is a more subtle deception with the same intended goal, but it's useless unless a high-numbered player slips up. An age-old proverb of con artists is that you can't con an honest person. In the Blind Partnership Game, you can't con a high-numbered player who follows the keep-your-own strategy.

Thus, if these low-number strategies are successful, they may be judged unethical; if they are unsuccessful, they are thought of as somewhere between crafty and devious. Neither strategy should work. High-numbered players who are victimized by these strategies may be quick to judge them unethical, not because the strategies are so bad, but because they themselves bargained poorly.

The Information Game.   Was I unethical when I bought the used car after returning from my sabbatical? In particular, was it ethical to use the following information to bargain toughly: (1) It was Christmastime when people may be short of money due to holiday expenses; and (2) the car had been advertised in the paper for at least two weeks. I prefer to think that it wasn't unethical, for the following reasons. (Another case of self-justification? You be the judge.)

First, I was honest and open in all my dealings with the owners. I didn't deceive them or falsify information in any way. I did not reveal the highest offer I would make for the car—but they didn't ask me this either. To be honest, I'm not sure what my highest offer would have been.

Second, I never had any specific information about this particular couple and whether they might be desperate to sell their car. In the end, I accepted their counteroffer. They may have dropped their estimate of what they could get for the car after getting no previous offers and finding me bargaining hard. But being tough is not unethical.

When I told this story to a businessman who happened to be sitting next to me on an airplane, he enjoyed it so much that I worried whether I really had bargained too well. He thought I had gotten a fantastic deal. Of course, I didn't tell him how much the European mechanic cost me before the purchase was really complete.

The other side of this coin is thinking that you might have paid too much for something. Take, for example, the story of a good friend who recently bought his first house. He was quite unsure whether he should try to buy it and asked me to have a look before he did anything. I thought that since he was hesitating and in no real hurry, he might wait and see whether other houses in the neighborhood would look better. But when I returned after being out of town the next week, he surprised me by saying he had bought it.

The house was originally listed at $63,500. (Home prices in central Illinois can be very low.) Since it needed a lot of work, he opened by offering $54,000. The old woman who owned the house told him she couldn't sell for that little. In talking about the house, where she had lived for fifty-seven years, she said, "Not a harsh word has ever been spoken under this roof." That didn't sound possible, but she was quite sincere. She also said that she needed at least $59,000. My friend finally agreed to $58,000.

He was worried that he had paid too much. "Do you think I could have bought the house for less?" I hemmed and hawed, because I thought he probably could have. He understood what I wasn't saying and said that he didn't want to take advantage of the old lady, and that his house payments weren't that much higher than they would have been if he had paid $55,000 or $56,000. He continues to wonder whether he should have bargained harder and paid less. But he also realizes that accepting the old lady's higher counteroffer hasn't cost him that much, and he was totally disarmed by her revelation about "never a harsh word."

In both the car and the house stories, a different bargaining process could have produced a substantially different selling price. But also, in both cases, it doesn't appear that any unethical behavior occurred.

In the Information Game, there was also the possibility for unethical behavior. In particular, when the $20 player asked the $500 player, "What's your prize?" the $500 player sometimes said that it was $20. That is a direct falsification and seems to be clearly unethical behavior. We've already discussed how it was strategically ineffective. The question then becomes, how can $500 players *not* reveal the value of their prize and *not* lie to the $20 players?

If they simply say that they didn't want to tell or that it didn't make any difference, they are implying that their prize was higher than $20. But if they say anything else, they are being deceptive. For instance, one response might be, "Not too high." Another might be "It's okay; nothing special." There are a host of other possibilities. Each tries to fend off additional questions while simultaneously providing no real information about the value of the $500 prize. Changing the discussion to another topic is a strategy that's less deceptive and can be very effective.

The moral is that if you ask a question and you don't get a specific answer, you might want to ask again until you do. If you still don't get an answer, you can probably conclude that the other person doesn't want to answer your question—and that implies that their answer might hurt their bargaining position.

The Ultimatum Game. The long story in Chapter 6 concerned Pat asking for $80,000 of the $100,000. It's easy to make a case that her request is ethical since she provided a reason that was both good enough to be convincing and also true. If what Pat had said wasn't good enough—for example if it was "I need a new house"—we wouldn't think the statement or the request was unethical, just strategically ineffective. Thus, whether a strategy is ethical depends primarily on truth. When your reason is a lie, we call it a falsification and most of the time label it unethical. We'll return to this a bit later.

Consider another "what if" in this situation. What if Pat had said, "I think we should try to equate our benefits in this deal. Since I'm so much richer than you, it will take more to make me happy. So I should get eighty thousand of the hundred thousand dollars and you should get twenty thousand—which will certainly make you very happy. Possibly even happier than I will be with an additional eighty thousand."

It may be a mind-boggling statement to hear, but is it unethical? Especially if Pat really believes it? Once again, we would argue that this is a strategic act that's not unethical if it represents true feelings. If it's only strategic and Pat would settle for $50,000, then it's incumbent on you to respond with an equally effective strategy to ensure that you each finish with $50,000.

There are many kinds of truth. As we have mentioned earlier, distinctions between the whole truth and something less than the whole truth are easy to make. What if Pat was not telling the truth about her mother's illness—but she needed the money to open a center for juvenile delinquents and knew that you would never agree if she used that as a reason? An ethical judgment here depends on whether you agree with the end that Pat has in mind—and whether you agree with the tactics. It's not an easy call.

The Battle of the Sexes. In the Battle of the Sexes, we alluded to the possibility that the husband may have introduced modern dance as an additional alternative not just to provide a compromise, but because he actually wanted to see it more than anything else. Thus, he not only came up with the idea, but he could also have misrepresented his preferences.

Let's assume that the husband was actually trying this bit of subterfuge. (If he was being open and honest, there is no ethical issue.) What would the immediate consequences of his act be? First, if he really enjoyed the show, he would have to tone down his expressions of enjoyment. If he was too happy about it, he would provide his wife with a clue that he had lied. So unless he could enjoy himself quietly, he would have to temper his reactions, which by itself might reduce his enjoyment of the show. In addition, he would have to hide his underhanded behavior from his wife forever. If they have shared an openly communicative, honest relationship over the years, this might be a very difficult task.

Thus, the husband would start paying for his act almost immediately. Factoring that into all the other possibilities might make this a very bad overall strategy. But what could the husband do instead? Ironically, telling the truth would give him a good case to go to the dance concert anyway. If the dance concert were her third choice and his first, it would compare very favorably with any of the other alternatives. By playing it down, then, as a compromise candidate, the husband might do worse than by telling the truth.

If modern dance were his fourth favorite alternative, however, that would push the blues bar into the compromise position. Thus, discovering an alternative that is worse than his third preference means he is worse off by suggesting it (assuming that his wife reacts with opposite preferences, as she has with all the others). Strategically, then, if he wants to increase his chances, he shouldn't suggest additional choices that he prefers less. But this borders on deception. Once again, we can conclude that, if they are close friends, they will want to maximize their joint gain, and their different preferences—and any concern about ethics—shouldn't be a big problem.

The crux of the ethics/trust stories is that bargainers must look for truth and do what they can to ensure that an agreement is binding, that violation of trust or unethical behavior is costly, and that trusting behavior and ethical action are rewarded.

THE RELEASE OF UNETHICAL BEHAVIOR

If you define someone's behavior as unethical, you may feel released to act unethically yourself. This is what I call the Domino Principle of No Ethics: Once it starts, conflict and vengeful behavior escalate.

A more scurrilous example of this vicious cycle can begin when one person expects the other to act unethically and is preemptively unethical. This is usually a self-fulfilling prophecy that initiates the domino effect. People who are very competitive may be the most likely to begin this chain reaction: They can be totally unaware that other bargainers may want to act cooperatively.

Another facilitator of unethical behavior is someone who will support an individual's unethical actions. Even the most competitive people may have self-doubts about the correctness of their behavior. If they find a colleague or a friend who validates their actions, they're home free. Thus, people who live alone may be less prone to unethical behavior than people who have housemates or spouses who will support what they do (especially when they hear only one side of the story).

Loners are more subject to remorse since they have no one to support their potentially unethical behaviors. If they have any doubts at all, it's hard to dispel them. Along these lines, Robyn Dawes of Carnegie-Mellon University tells a story about an experiment he ran at an old people's home. Twenty people participated; all were required to publicly announce whether they would choose A (the cooperative choice) or B (the noncooperative choice). If everyone cooperated, they would all win a small monetary prize. If one person didn't and the rest did, the defector would win a large prize and the others would win less. As with all social dilemmas, the game provided people with a temptation to defect while also providing the highest joint benefit when everyone cooperated.

Everyone in the group announced that they would choose cooperatively. After that, they made their actual choices privately; they were paid privately, too. Everyone cooperated but one.

The next morning, when Robyn reached his office, he found several phone messages, all asking him to call a man at the old people's home. When he made the call, an older gentleman explained that he couldn't sleep at all the previous night. He had played the game the previous day and, since he was a recently retired stock broker, "he couldn't help but see the possibilities. Was there any way he could give the money back?"

CONCLUSION

Bargaining games are breeding grounds for unethical behavior. Temptations abound. Private information is typical, and information is guarded and prized. Individualistic motives conflict with the collective good; what's good for one is rarely good for the other. Competition seems to be many people's strategy of first choice. Everyone may perceive different outcomes as fair. Sharing, exploring, and trusting are cooperative but risky strategies. When unethical acts or competition are successful, people may incorrectly generalize and be continually competitive and fall into actions with questionable ethics.

Are bargaining games an ethical quagmire? They certainly can be. When you're not bargaining with friends, it pays to be careful, to establish contractual agreements, to penalize unethical behavior, to publicize what you expect, and to reward ethical conduct. Being fair is riskier and requires protection.

Friendship and trust can facilitate cooperation. Nevertheless, expectations of what's appropriate need to be shared—explicitly—even among trusted friends. Unfulfilled expectations can be identified as unethical behavior, which can ruin trust *and* friendship. Thus, the risk when you're negotiating with a friend is much greater: There's more to lose than just a deal. This can happen when both friends truly feel they are acting ethically, in ways that they think the other person expects. So even when you're bargaining with friends, it pays to be careful and, in big transactions, to get things down in writing.

To say there's a moral to the story of ethics is a pleasant irony. In fact, there are several morals. They're all a reflection of simple common sense, but they bear repeating since they may increase the probability that we will put them into action.

1. Learn from your mistakes. Almost everyone has been unsuccessful in totally avoiding ethical mistakes in their bargaining behaviors.

2. Look at yourself in the mirror and ask whether you like what you see. It's hard to hide from yourself after you've acted unethically. If you don't like what you see in the mirror, do as much as you can to undo whatever you did, and then refer to number 1.

3. Put yourself in others' shoes and see how they see you. If their picture is a good one, you're probably doing fine.

If you have only satisfied your needs and not theirs, your negotiations should not be over, whether you want them to be or not.

4. Be on guard. To be fair, ethical, and cooperative is rarely the simplest strategy. As we've seen, though, it can pay both personal and social dividends.

GAMES' END

You have decided that it's time to buy a new car. You've kept your eyes open lately and think you know what you want. In fact, there's one model that has really caught your eye. You can't help being excited about the possibility of actually owning and driving this car.

You decide to check it out with a dealer. The test drive is just fine—it really feels good. As you expected, however, the price is not as low as you would like it to be.

This example is identical to the one that starts this book. The example continues: "After some haggling (and possibly checking out a few other cars), you make the deal and buy the car. You feel a great rush—what a car!"

Now, however, you should be taking a different approach to bargaining. Each chapter gave you some bargaining tools, for buying a car or negotiating anything. As we review this material, we'll see how it applies to this recurring example.

First and foremost, you should know yourself. While reading this book, you have had an opportunity to project yourself into the games to see how you would react. By reflecting back on your reactions, you should have a pretty good picture of yourself as a general negotiator. Before buying a car, you should know yourself in three ways: as a person, as a bargainer, and as the person bargaining for this particular car. You should know how much you want it and how much you would spend to have it. You should formulate target and resistance prices—before you find out the car's price—because we know how easy it is to be affected by the stated prices.

You should know the strategies you'll be able to use and be comfortable with. You might consider a take-it-or-leave-it offer if you want to avoid a long bargaining process. At the other extreme, you might formulate a plan for multiple trips to the dealer, hoping to soften up the salesperson each time and eventually get the best deal possible. You might also plan how you can use hypotheticals to reach the most integrative agreement possible.

Second, you should know your opponent. You don't need to delve into her family history. But you might try to find other people who have bought cars from her before. Knowing her tendencies can be invaluable. In addition, this feeds back into knowing yourself, since you need to know who you will be when you bargain with this particular person.

You can formulate the best strategies if you can put yourself into her shoes. By mentally switching roles before you begin (and during negotiation), you can begin to understand what the seller would like to hear from you. This advice is as old as the hills, and obvious, too. But the fact that few people consciously do this means it's worth repeating. Visualizing yourself bargaining is hard enough; visualizing your opponents and how they will bargain is even harder. Thus, it's easy to say that you should put yourself in the other person's shoes; it's still hard to put this advice into effective practice.

Third, you must carefully consider the bargaining situation. Do they have a quota they must meet at the end of the month, making them more open to a deal on the twenty-ninth or thirtieth rather than the first or second? Do they have a large inventory that they need to move quickly—particularly on the model you are interested in? Do they offer a warranty that's comparable to those of other dealers, and if they don't, is it negotiable? Clearly, there are limits to how much information you can get or even how much information you want. You should weigh your time and effort against the chances of getting additionally valuable information. But there's one thing to remember: Most people don't get enough information before, during, or after bargaining.

Strategy number four is to identify prominent solutions whenever you can. Round numbers are always prominent, so a list price between $20,000 and $25,000 would probably lead to $20,000 being prominent. As the price gets lower, there are more prominent possibilities, with any amount that's divisible by 1,000 being prominent for prices less than $12,000 or so. Between $12,000 and $20,000, prominent figures might include $13,000, $15,000, $16,000, or $18,000. By knowing what's prominent, you can formulate your strategy *backward,* from the most likely final result to your first strategic moves. When you or your opponent get off the right track, you can push things back on. Knowing the structure of the situation and how it can generate a prominent solution can be very handy information that helps you get what you want.

Fifth, you should pay close attention to the salesperson's nonverbals. They may give you a better read on how she feels about your proposals and about her own counteroffers. Sweaty palms, an unexpected flush, beating around the bush—any sign of discomfort—can mean that you are pushing things effectively. But nonverbals are often difficult to interpret accurately. In particular, salespeople try not to give anything away. But if you negotiate for a long time with the same person, it's hard for them not to leak something revealing.

As we've noted, nonverbals are most illuminating when they conflict with what someone is saying. So by also keeping track of someone's verbal statements, you have a better chance of learning whether they're trying to do something on the sly. The man who sold me the funky bag in the Old City in Jerusalem didn't give anything away nonverbally. It was only his words, "It's very old," that clued me in. So words and nonwords both deserve your attention. You'll do much better when you keep your eyes and ears open.

Strategy number six is to be exploratory—especially when the chances that you will get hurt and the costs you might incur are low. If another dealer can sell you the same car, you can bargain hard and explore all the possibilities with the first dealer. Strong, competitive negotiating can be successful, in the short run. If you are buying the car in a big city where you are one of many, many potential customers, and the dealer will never know who you are, you should probably bargain very hard, always realizing that you want to maximize what you want out of the bargain, whether it is price or good feelings or self-respect. In a small town, however, the long run can be much more important, and being overly competitive can poison your reputation. Any gains you might achieve from early competitive action can soon disappear.

The most difficult situations, of course, are those that fall between these two extremes, where you can get a bad deal if you don't bargain hard but you don't want to ruin your reputation by being too competitive. There are also the difficult situations where trying to be cooperative simultaneously risks big losses if your opponent does not reciprocate. These are the times with a high potential for nice guys to finish last. Slowing down the negotiations can give you an idea whether the other side is likely to be trustworthy or cooperative. You might also be able to fragment your first strategic moves so that smaller, less costly actions can come first. By being professional in your actions, respecting your own position and that of the other bargainer, you can bargain hard and bargain honorably. Knowing your opponent is critical here, too, because it's your opponent's perceptions that can determine your reputation.

You can *always* use more information (strategy number seven). A good decision maker is constantly open to new information, and good decision makers make for better bargainers.

You can also release information that's advantageous to you. When I bought my first new car, I was young and naive, but I knew enough to shop around at several dealers. Although I didn't do it on purpose, I left their trade-in offers on the front seat of the car, and whenever a new dealer looked at my old car, he knew the price he had to beat. This example also emphasizes the importance of alternatives: If you have your heart set on only one car, and there is only one dealer who can sell it to you, you will probably have to pay a lot for it. If you can buy it from another dealer, you will have considerably more leverage when you bargain with the first dealer.

If you have information that's advantageous to the other person (for example, you just got some windfall profits from a stock purchase and you can easily afford this car), you have two basic choices: (1) Ignore it, bargain hard, and do as well as you would have if the profits didn't exist; or (2) use your information to formulate a fair agreement and work to put it into effect. The first alternative is difficult: Only the most effective bargainers can ignore information. The second alternative is also difficult: Your opponent may not understand that you are actually promoting a fair agreement. Research suggests that bargaining reasonably but less forcefully can lead to your opponent bargaining harder. It is just like the story in the first chapter about bargaining for crafts in Latin America: You don't want to fold immediately even when something beautiful costs next to nothing. You should do some serious bargaining to communicate that you are an able, serious negotiator, but you don't need to go overboard and bargain for more than you really want.

In a perfect world, you and your car dealer would exchange information freely and problem-solve your way to an agreement. You would get an acceptable deal and the dealer would make a reasonable profit. You would discover a good solution rather than getting into tough negotiating. If this were possible—if everyone understood that problem solving can provide far superior outcomes, and if everyone could trust each other and be cooperative—we'd be much closer to that perfect world.

Eighth, you should propose an agreement that is fair, even when you are negotiating with a car dealer. If you are bargaining for a new car, you can find out the dealer's cost ahead of time. Offering him less than he had to pay for the car obviously makes no sense. But offering him enough to cover his additional costs and provide him with some profit does make complete sense.

This extends the put-yourself-in-the-other-person's-shoes directive. Here, you need to take your opponents' point of view and, essentially, propose an agreement that they will ultimately accept. This may not give you your best possible outcome, but it increases your chances for actually reaching an agreement—which can be worlds better than no agreement. If you didn't reach an agreement with one dealer, for instance, and had to turn to the only other dealer in the area, you would have lost the advantage of having an alternative. Especially if this last dealer knows that he is your last option, you probably won't be able to get such a good deal.

This means that, to reach an agreement, you may not be getting a rock-bottom, minimum price. This is not to say that you will accept a price that you can't afford, but you may pay a bit more than you really wanted to. A small, short-term sacrifice, however, can be very effective: You reach agreement quicker and can move on to other negotiations and other positive outcomes. Accumulating many small payoffs may also pay greater dividends than a few large ones.

If precedents are involved (that is, if you will be buying cars from the same person repeatedly), you may have to protect your reputation *and* not settle for less. Again, this is where it pays to be professional and persistent. Finding the fine line between not doing badly yourself and not having the other bargainer do badly takes skill and patience, knowledge of their limits, and openness to protracted negotiations.

Precedents are also an issue in very competitive negotiations when you're faced with an ultimatum. If your reaction could put you in position to be taken advantage of over and over, you won't want to make any sacrifices. On the other hand, an emotional reaction may leave you out in the cold. If you were actually in a situation where your friend Pat asked for $80,000 of the $100,000, for instance, and this would make you angry, you might both get nothing and be even angrier. Thus, both precedents and emotions must be considered carefully in the face of an ultimatum.

Our ninth recommendation is to beware of threats, whether you make them or receive them. If you make a threat and the other person responds in kind, you may find yourself in a dangerous Game of Chicken. You'll be less likely to reach an agreement, whether it's buying a car or anything else. If you do reach agreement, you may lose any chance for positive postnegotiation benefits, which in the case of a new purchase might mean losing out on dependable service.

If both of you are stubborn, if your threats are public, or if you're worried that your credibility will be shot if you recant, it may be very difficult to back down after someone has made a threat. As a result, both of you may end up getting your worst possible outcomes. Chicken is a dangerous game. It pays to try not to play. Making a threat or responding with a second threat opens a door that you would probably prefer to keep closed. So, again, beware of threats. And whatever else you do, avoid playing the original Game of Chicken.

Tenth, you can always expect some conflict, even in the best of interactions. Different people have different ideas—almost by definition—about bargaining, about what's ethical, about anything. Identical twins may have identical preferences for many things, but if one is selling a car to the other, they'll be coming at the deal from different directions and may have different ideas about the sale. The best of friends have differences of opinion, too. That doesn't diminish their friendship. Instead, it simply means that work is always part of successful relationships. Conflict only becomes a real problem if you don't work for a solution.

But it does pay to bargain with your friends. You know them better than you know anyone else. It's much more pleasant dealing with them than bargaining with strangers or enemies! In fact, when we are interacting with friends we usually don't feel like we're bargaining. Instead, we usually think of it as normal, everyday interaction. When we're with friends, we can be free with our information and our preferences. We don't need to calculate and strategize. Instead, we simply have to open up and make sure all the important issues are raised and discussed—if they need to be raised and discussed in the first place. If we are buying a car from a friend, we can be pretty sure of a fair price and a fair deal. At the same time, if you are selling a car to a friend, you may not get the highest price for it, but you also may avoid all the hassles that go with selling it to a stranger.

Joint negotiating to buy a car is another effective strategy if you and your cobuyer coordinate well. One of you can play the good guy, for instance, while the other plays the bad guy. By coordinating you can do better than either of you might alone. The flip side comes when your strategies are not coordinated—then you may undercut each other and give the seller a real advantage.

Strategy number eleven is to forget sunk costs. Many sellers use the bait-and-hook strategy, advertising something at the lowest possible price, and then revealing the costs of all the "extras" when you have already made the trip to the showroom. Getting there is a relatively small investment, especially in relation to the price of the car, but it's also a cost that you have already incurred. What can be more substantial is the emotional investment you make when you finally decide to buy the car. To finally be able to say yes to a deal, you have probably resolved a number of concerns and uncertainties, and this resolution process may present considerable effort. In days gone by (and still today?), some car sellers recognized this investment, and after you said yes but before the final contract was signed, extra, hidden charges all of a sudden appeared. Many people succumbed and paid the extra charges, possibly because they had already invested so much of themselves into the decision and didn't want to back out.

If you ignore costs that are sunk, you have a better chance of avoiding dysfunctional escalation or being susceptible to questionable bargaining practices. But it's hard to realize that, once you have invested money, effort, or time, your investments are *irretrievable*—they can't be redeemed or resurrected. They're gone. This truth is physical, not mental: These investments don't disappear from our minds. We identify personally with what we've done—and we let it affect our future actions. It's as if we're bound by our previous behavior and have little freedom to deny it or act any differently.

Rationally, of course, sunk costs are sunk and we should act without concern for what we've already invested. Just as it pays to be cool and calm when we're bargaining and not let our emotions determine our actions, it's also important to take a forward- rather than backward-looking orientation in bargaining. Learning from past behavior is important. Letting it control our current actions and future outcomes can be totally ineffective. As with emotions, however, following this advice is much easier said than done.

Our twelfth strategy is to avoid doing anything now that will feel bad later. Giving in to a seller's demands, just to get him or her to stop bothering you, can lead to regret later on. Thus, before you make a choice that commits you to an action or an expense, you might transport yourself into the near future (in your mind) and look back on the present. If the picture looks bleak, you might want to reconsider your strategies. Acting too quickly, being impatient, or losing your cool are all too easy.

Volunteering—doing anything more than the minimum necessary—may mean that you and the seller will reach a jointly pleasing deal. Everyone may benefit, even though you did more—and almost any act of volunteering presents this possibility. Knowing this in advance can reduce some of volunteering's potentially negative emotional baggage, but thoughts of inequity often endure, especially if your counterpart strays from your expectations. It's particularly difficult, for instance, to forget the combination of your own magnanimity and his apparent greed. Considering how you will feel after a negotiation is over—before you have made your final choices—gives you a better chance of making the right decisions and avoiding unnecessary regret.

Strategy number thirteen: Be careful in auctions. If the car you are buying is one of a kind, you must know how important it is to you before you bid. You must keep your emotions in check. When there are many bidders, you should guard against letting their interests sway you to bid more than you want to, although their expressed value for the car may increase your evaluation of it, too. If you are uncertain about the car's objective value, you should probably discount your subjective evaluation, too. All these recommendations are rational rather than psychological, and again, they are easier said than done.

The time before an auction is not only valuable for inspecting the car but also for inspecting your own feelings. It's critical to coolly evaluate an object and identify the highest price you would pay for it, before the bidding begins. It can help anchor your future bids and limit the chances that you will be influenced by everyone else's interest.

On the one hand, it's rational to keep your emotions in check and not get carried away. On the other, the emotions of bidding can be a real thrill—one that too much rationality might prevent you from experiencing. Thus, the thrill of bidding might also enter into your calculations when you determine your maximum price. To be comprehensive in your strategy formulations, you might also consider the thrill of paying a low price for a valuable car and how it compares with the risk of paying too much for a car that's less valuable than you had hoped.

When we think more globally, rather than individually, we may realize that helping our community (however we define it) can have long-run positive effects for us as well. Thus, buying a car in the neighborhood, even if you pay slightly more, may be an added cost in the short run but a gain in the long run. Your supportive action can help resolve the inherent dilemma of group (community) action. By contributing locally (strategy number fourteen), you implicitly encourage everyone else to contribute, too. By buying a car produced in your own country and sold in your own neighborhood, you contribute and cooperate rather than defect and compete. It helps solve the problems of social dilemmas.

We know that people are much more willing to cooperate when they know that others will, too. By increasing the probability of some others contributing, you may start a cooperation snowball, with people being even more willing to cooperate. Once things get rolling, there's nothing like a bandwagon of cooperators to encourage others to hop on and cooperate, too. Whether you moralize, restrict group size, or increase the payoffs for mutual cooperation, increasing everyone's identification within the community is another excellent step toward unanimous cooperation.

Whatever you do, don't hesitate to negotiate (number fifteen). Bargaining can create benefits for you and the seller. By working hard to take advantage of the integrative potential of an interaction, everyone can win. Explore the possibilities;

search for creative solutions. Bargain hard and be as fair as you can be. This is not the same as being destructively competitive. You should push the situation, rather than the other bargainer, for all its worth.

Finally, it pays to act ethically—even with a car dealer. Although there are always people who will support and reinforce questionable, even unethical behavior, it's hard to get away from mirrors. Self-doubts inevitably accompany unethical behavior, as does the risk of a ruined reputation. Fair, ethical conduct is personally and societally effective.

As you become a more adept bargainer, you should know which strategies you might use in any particular situation. At the same time, you should expand your ability to diagnose different situations. When your intuition is correct, you can immediately focus on a small set of effective strategies and choose the best strategy for (1) you, (2) the situation, and (3) the other people involved. You should now be prepared to negotiate a wide variety of bargaining games—many more than the specific games that we have presented here.

We are now nearing the end of the book. A few last words are in order. Chapter 1 ended with some rules of thumb. I've incorporated some of them in this last chapter's recommendations, including the rules to know yourself and to know the situation. I have reiterated a few of the others, like doing as well as you can for yourself and staying cool and calm and acting professionally. Working within your own position was initially geared toward dealing with power, but it could be expanded to emphasize how important knowing yourself really is. It pays to avoid blindly competitive urges, to act strategically, and to learn from what has happened. In the end, the rules all boil down to three overall strategies:

Know yourself.
Know the other(s).
Know the situation.

When you know all three, and you know what to do with this knowledge, you can negotiate extremely well. This sounds very easy. The paradox of bargaining is that all this knowing takes a lot of effort and well-conceived strategies.

This, then, is the end of *Bargaining Games*. It's not an endgame, which is the final set of moves in a game of chess. It's not land's end, where a piece of geography juts off into a body of water. But it is the end of this book and, I hope, the point where your negotiations get better and better.